The Art of Swimming

Steven Shaw & Armand D'Angour

The Art of Swimming

*a new direction using
the Alexander Technique*

Foreword by Victoria Wood

Ashgrove Publishing
London & Bath

'The Art of Swimming', could easily be titled 'The Joy of Swimming'. With Shaw and D'Angour's approach to swimming, I broke up my tension-producing habits and discovered a sense of joy and pleasure in moving through the water. For me, as a self-taught swimmer who has used other instructional books for guidance, it is the most sensible and rewarding approach to swimming in print.
Glenn Kenreich, American Society of Alexander Technique Teachers

Shaw's Method is very effective in improving body awareness in the water. It helps elite athletes to be aware of where they are in the water, and helps recreational swimmers to avoid discomfort and sore muscles and be more absorbed in what they are doing.
Paul Massey, British Olympics physiotherapist

Having been a physiotherapist for more than thirty years, there have been many occasions where I've wanted to recommend swimming to patients. But I have been worried about the damage they may do to themselves if they are not swimming correctly. If they swim using this approach, the can learn the benefits of pain-free swimming.
Gillian Jordan, Principal Lecturer, University of Greenwich

We are happy with the application of the Alexander Technique to swimming, we are very aware of the fear response which creates tension in swimmers, and we are also very much in agreement that the spine should be kept aligned throughout strokes.
Gart Seaghers, Development Co-ordinator,
Swimming Teachers Association

Shaw and D'Angour are to be commended for their work in pioneering an approach to the teaching of swimming based on the Alexander Technique.
Jonathon Drake, Alexander Journal

The method has redefined the art of swimming much in the same as the PADI approach has redefined the art of scuba diving. We applaud its contribution and vision
Drew Richardson, PADI Worldwide

Contents

foreword by
Victoria Wood

I was taught to swim at the age of ten in Bury Baths in Lancashire by a woman holding a pole and shouting. I could do a length of strained breast stroke and I could also do what was described on my certificate as a 'Simple Dive'. Really it was more of a panicked flop.

At secondary school I swam once a week. I loved the water but I never felt at ease in it. We spent a lot of time diving for bricks and treading water in our pyjamas, obviously readying ourselves for some incident similar to the sinking of the Titanic. A big annual highlight was the Swimming Gala, where we waited eagerly for the Long Plunge. This was invariably won by an enormous girl in a pink chequered costume, who floated interminably like a piece of living Battenburg.

In my twenties I would sometimes pootle about in a grubby old-fashioned pool, but mainly I just fantasised about exercise, and didn't do any. I tried a thing that fastened to the doorknob that was supposed to give you a stomach like an ironing board, but I lost enthusiasm when someone opened the door and concussed me.

I started to swim again. I worked up from two lengths to twenty and painfully did twenty lengths every time I went to a pool. I did that terrible contorted breast stroke you see so often, head half out of the water, spine scrunched up, eyes fixed desperately on the clock, praying for 'getting out time'.

Then a friend taught me how to do the breathing for crawl, and I loved the feel of that once I got the knack. I bought goggles and a racing costume, which were a great improvement. It meant I could swim without getting sore eyes or whacking an old age pensioner in the eye with an escaping bosom. I upgraded myself to forty lengths and did it every weekday for about two years. Doggedly and never showing any improvement, I did a 35 mile round trip, with forty lengths in the middle of it, day after day

Of course, it became mind-numbingly boring, apart from the other disadvantages like always stinking of chlorine, and going around for part of the day with someone's old corn plaster stuck on my elbow. I would plough up and down, always doing crawl, because that was all I was comfortable with, never varying the routine. I would sometimes try and increase the pace, and would thrash harder and kick faster and yet not move through the water any quicker.

So I gave up on swimming. I did aerobics and weights and rubber bands and step and found that exercise could go hand in hand with enjoyment. But always, nagging at the back of my mind, was this feeling that I should be able to swim for fitness; and that if only I was told properly what to do, I would be able to get the joy that should be there for us when we're in the water.

I would love to be able to move through that element with the confidence I have when exercising on land. I do see now that that deadly unvarying forty lengths is not a good, effective or enjoyable way to exercise. There are a lot of people, like me, who know enough to swim but not enough to hold themselves correctly or train effectively for everyday fitness. Although I already knew Steven because he teaches one of my children swimming, I can honestly say that this book is one I would have bought anyway. I want to know how to move in the water in the right way; I want swimming to be a joy and not a chore or a penance. I want wet fun and if this book doesn't help me get it then I'm popping on my chequered swimming costume and going out for a Long Plunge.

authors' foreword
to the second edition

*With the right mental approach experiences may be encountered which are
normally associated with the practice of yoga, tai chi and meditation...
it is interesting to speculate how the art of swimming would be
regarded now if hitherto unfamiliar to Western Culture,
it had been introduced from the East only within
the last few decades.*
Dr Mike Hobdell

The Art of Swimming originated in a desire to articulate a new direction for
swimmers and non-swimmers alike. The authors' perspectives on swimming were
widely different. One was an inveterate non-swimmer who was delighted to discover a love of swimming after having dismissed the prospect altogether. The
other, Steven, was a swimming instructor and a former competitive swimmer
whose enthusiasm for swimming had vanished until he began to apply principles
of the Alexander Technique to water activity. We both had many years' experience
of the Technique and recognised how it could offer an approach to swimming
which embraced a fuller exploration of the crucial psychophysical dimensions so
often overlooked by swimming teachers. The effects of fear, the difficulty of
breathing, the body's orientation in water, and the consequences of over-
competitiveness: these were the things which seemed to us vital to think about
in learning to swim and doing so with pleasure. In writing *The Art of Swimming*
we sought to give them due consideration, and to question received doctrines
which had failed us both. But in particular, we wanted to investigate how the art
of swimming might be illuminated by the principles of the Alexander Technique
– and how, in turn, the Technique might be reconsidered from the perspective of
water activity.

Since its appearance in 1996 the book has attracted considerable acclaim. *The
Art of Swimming* has been read by swimmers ranging from complete beginners
to competitive athletes, and its warm reception reflects the enthusiasm with
which it was written. After numerous reprints, the pressure for a new edition has

become irresistible. We have not sought to change the core message. The book was never intended to be either an instruction manual or a scientific statement of swimming technique. Its basic aims were to suggest new ways of relating to water and to offer a productive re-orientation of the whole notion of swimming. We hoped to inspire swimmers at all levels to further their individual exploration and understanding of water. Everyone can find something to learn from this approach, whatever their aims and level of attainment in swimming.

With this edition we have sought to bring the book up-to-date and to enhance its appearance, but we have also made substantial changes where further thought, experience, and input from readers have indicated the need to restate, develop or elaborate our ideas. While the book is not intended to be a substitute for practical swimming instruction, persistent requests from readers have led us to incorporate more specific suggestions for useful practices for mastering the strokes. Those seeking tips on improving specific aspects of stroke technique may now refer to the fuller Stroke Guides and to the Helpful Hints sections. However, the book is not designed or intended as a continuous programme of instruction or a definitive guide to practice – because the process of learning is fluid, individual, and endless, and the art of swimming requires a continuing creative exploration of our relationship to water.

introduction

When we have no thought of achievement,
no thought of self, we are true beginners.
This is also the real secret of the arts:
always be a beginner.
Shunryu Suzuki

Can swimming be an *art*? In this book, we question the conventional view of
swimming as a *sport* in which the prime requirements are strength and determination, and where higher levels of proficiency may be attained through a focus
on physical fitness. Such an approach sets up pre-defined goals, in particular the
attainment of speed. Swimming in a competitive context is about swimming
fast, which involves knowing how to manoeuvre through the water with maximum efficiency. But at its best, the efficiency of a good swimmer's technique
cannot be divorced from artistic style. It is elegant because it is effective, and it
works because it is beautiful. Good swimming attracts praise for its aesthetic
qualities. Great swimmers – dolphins as well as Olympic medallists – are notable
for qualities of gracefulness, flow and economy of movement. As in a great
picture or piece of music, there is a sense of completeness about a lovely swimming style. Nothing seems out of place or redundant. The fine swimmer is a
natural artist in the water.

Few handbooks exist that can inspire adults, whether swimmers or non-
swimmers, to learn effective swimming skills. Instructional books tend to focus
on methods for swimming *faster or further*, rather than on *swimming well and
enjoying the water*. When technique is discussed it is often couched in language
which, in the words of US coach Terry Laughlin, 'makes efficient swimming
sound like rocket science.' High-level competitive swimming – the model on
which most swimming teaching is based – is presented as fighting a battle
against an intransigent opponent. Swimming coaches even talk about water as
the 'wall': one which can only be broken through by ease and guile, because it
certainly cannot be attacked head-on.

Fighting with the water is one perspective. Many swimmers do it without
realising it. But water will never allow us to do what it cannot do for us.
Co-operating with it, exploring our relationship to it, understanding and valuing

its qualities, can be the basis of a far more productive approach, one which we emphasise throughout this book. Whether water is to be treated as a hostile opponent or a generous ally is a matter for us to decide for ourselves. If we know how, we can derive marvellous benefits from its properties of buoyancy, fluidity, and density – the properties that allow us to float, to flow, and to swim.

Swimming is not just about manoeuvring oneself through the water. It is also about being *in* water and *with* water. There is an art just to being in the water which is rarely associated with common conceptions of swimming, and has much more to do with the *quality* of the experience. When swimming is approached as an art, rather than a technique, a science, or a means to fitness, it takes on a whole new dimension. First of all, the whole motivation for the swimmer changes. The emphasis is not on getting there faster, or on winning a race against other swimmers for a pre-ordained reward. Its significance becomes less narrow and more exploratory. The reward is not an object presented at the end of a race, but is present in the very process of exploration and in the pleasure of enhanced awareness in the water.

Art involves skill, but occupies a wider domain than skill. Doing something with art means discovering the peculiar excellence appropriate to the activity. Whereas activities are often undertaken for narrow practical ends, art exists for an abundance of reasons and purposes. Its goals may be the imitation of nature, as in painting and sculpture, or the pursuit of beauty, rhythm, and harmony, as in music or poetry. The symbolic qualities of art overlap in different media: a picture can have rhythm just as a dance can, and music expresses moods and colours as does a visual medium. Art is both self-expression and communication. It may involve the challenge of grappling with a physical medium to produce something that transcends pure physicality. Its deepest source is a part of our mind that does not reason, yet has a logic of its own. It has meanings that seek to be articulated but cannot be pinned down by words. Ultimately, art exists in itself and for itself.

How does the Alexander Technique encourage the swimmer to view swimming as an art? By giving us a closer understanding and appreciation of the working of the self. This awareness empowers us to think and act creatively, helping to set us free from the constraints of our automatic responses. As a result we can approach the water with a new sense of exploration, and discover a living, continuously unfolding relationship with it which goes beyond static, fixed ideas and conventional instruction. As our awareness is wakened to the way we move and function, we enter new realms of possibility for developing and exploring ourselves and our world. The Technique points us in the direction of thinking and acting in a freer, more balanced and integrated way – a key to the art of living itself.

A creative approach to the water is part of a creative approach to life. Age-old as well as new-age philosophies emphasise that truth is in the here and now. Too often, we grasp the kernel of this thought and twist it to derive tangible, egotistic profit from the truth it embodies. Yoga, for instance, is promoted as a way of getting fitter, slimmer, and stronger, and meditation is practised as a means to financial success, or to 'win friends and influence people'. Whatever the validity of these aims, can we draw back from such a narrowly goal-oriented approach? Thoughtful interaction with the water offers a possibility, because it encourages us to drop the focus on cultivating our ego and compels us to accept a deeper, truer, less subjective reality. Water cannot be tamed. It doesn't care how fast we swim, how hard we try, or how badly we want to succeed. It ebbs, flows, and swells regardless. What it seems to do to us is a reflection of what we do to ourselves. It will support us if we let it, resist us if we fight it, and frighten us if we approach it with fear. It is unconquerable because it does nothing, seeks nothing, needs nothing – it just *is*.

This book follows the natural flow of ideas which connect the Alexander Technique with the swimmer's art. The central chapters also contain Stroke Guides with practical suggestions for exploring and improving your strokes. Chapter 1, *The Wakening of Awareness*, describes the origins and key principles of the Technique, and outlines how they can be applied to learning to swim. The second chapter tackles rarely addressed issues regarding psychological barriers to swimming, and indicates the positive path to being *At Home in the Water*. Chapters 3 and 4 develop core aspects of the Alexander Technique with crucial implications for the art of swimming: *The Art of Breathing* and *Leading with the Head*. The fifth chapter explores how we tend to view and perform fitness activities, and suggests an alternative approach from the cautionary perspective that *Fitness Can Damage Your Health*. The last chapter concludes with reflections on water, the element which inspires the art of swimming but ultimately leads us *Beyond the Art of Swimming*.

chapter one

the wakening of awareness

*Self-knowledge is not a thing to be bought in books. Nor is it
the outcome of a long, painful practice or discipline,
but it is awareness from moment to moment of
every thought and feeling as it arises.*
Krishnamurti

Take a look at the swimmers in Figure 1.1. The bored expression, the bared teeth, the timid paddle. Swimmers like this can be seen in swimming-pools any day of the week. Where are those carefree, elegant swimmers who manifestly love the water and are such a pleasure to watch? They seem to be out of the frame. Is this, then, what swimming is all about – boredom, strain and discomfort? Non-swimmers can settle back in their chairs with a sigh of relief – they are obviously not missing anything. Yet… are you that non-swimmer? Do you, perhaps, recognise something of yourself in any of these caricatures? There's a good chance, of course, that the very swimmers on whom these characters are modelled would not recognise themselves, because they are all lacking in the same respect: a true and full awareness of what they are doing.

We limit our awareness in different ways. The awareness of the here and now, when we're doing something and enjoying every minute of it, is clearly not the experience of the figure on the left. His

Fig. 1.1

mind is on other things – the week-end, the ball-game – anything but what he's actually doing. Then there's the awareness that depends on knowledge: knowing how to use one's body in breaststroke, or knowing why swimming with one's head held stiffly out of the water is not a good idea. The young woman on the right of the cartoon obviously reckons that swimming is good exercise as long as she keeps her hair dry (*Fig. 1.1*). And there's the awareness of keeping a perspective on whatever we do, since the way we behave exemplifies our wider approach to life. Do we know when our lives lack balance, and do we know how to redress the balance? The figure in the centre is all too familiar. Jaw clenched, heedless of other swimmers, he strains his taut muscles against the water in an ungainly butterfly stroke, his sole aim to cut a half-second off his length. What more has he to learn? Everything, in our view, about the *art* of swimming.

Fig. 1.2   *The goals of competitive swimming rarely include having fun*

It's often said that swimming is the ideal type of exercise, the best way of exercising the whole body in a medium where the risk of injury is minimal. It supposedly combines the pleasure of a sport with the benefits of fitness. But the fact remains that many people don't associate swimming with pleasure, and even those who swim out of choice often seem to lack any sense of fun. They struggle through the water, their heads pulled back and their faces set in a grimace, their overriding

15

purpose being to complete a fixed number of laps in a given time. They act as if the water were an assault course which must be battled through from a sense of duty, rather than for pleasure or profit. Unaware of other swimmers around them, they seem oblivious even to the nature of their own experience. Those who swim regularly in this way are convinced that at least it's doing them good. But how much good can it do if their attention is focussed on something other than swimming – speed, fitness, or whatever? If our mind isn't engaged in what we're doing, the benefits of exercise are limited or non-existent. And what a waste of time if we can't even enjoy it.

Why is it that so many swimmers merely go through the motions rather than savour the quality of their experience? Why don't we discover how to enjoy swimming more than we do? One reason is that enjoying the water is usually taken for granted in swimming-teaching. Swimming instruction traditionally focusses on ways of moving the arms and legs, on techniques for swimming faster and longer, or on ploughing up and down a pool for extended periods of time. How we *think and feel* about swimming (and even what we think *about* when we swim) is generally ignored. But these aspects can be crucial – especially if our feelings are negative, as they often are. Fear, for instance, or boredom, which are feelings that many people associate with swimming, are rarely dealt with in a knowledgeable and constructive way. Yet such attitudes are widespread, and knowing how to deal with them will clearly have an important bearing on our relationship to the water.

For this reason, the teaching of swimming should always pay due attention to how we think and feel about water. If it doesn't, it overlooks the intimate connection between thought and action. The dissociation of the physical and the mental is commonplace in our scientific age. But while it can be hard to avoid talking about these domains as if they were quite separate, in doing so we create a mistaken and unhelpful impression. This gets in the way of our resolving the difficulties we may

Fig. 1.3
F.M. Alexander in his 70s

have in learning how to perform activities which require physical skill, and misleads teachers into neglecting an invaluable resource: the mind's ability to direct the body.

Many swimmers, for instance, don't recognise that specific problems in swimming relate to unresolved anxieties. But it takes only a moment's consideration to realise that swimmers at all levels can be affected by them. Such feelings are bound not only to detract from our ability to swim, but also to hinder any real potential to derive pleasure from the water. Traditional swimming lessons encourage us to divorce our mental processes from the physical activity in hand – rather than, say, to acknowledge our fears and to learn to overcome their inevitable side-effects. In blocking out thoughts and feelings about what we are trying to learn, we deliberately approach the learning experience with less than total sensitivity. We thus obstruct a vital aspect of our organic mind-body awareness – in short, of our *self*.

Because brain and body processes are in fact inseparable, the way we think and feel in and about ourselves is the foundation for our development as swimmers. A truly effective approach to swimming should therefore begin by appreciating the unity of the self – which is the basis of the Alexander Technique. Built on the principle of developing *self-awareness in action*, the Technique is a system of psychophysical re-education – a means of increasing our control over the way we act and think. Applied to swimming, it starts by prompting us to an awareness of how our thoughts affect our actions in the water, an awareness which furnishes the swimmer with valuable tools for learning. It encourages us to discover our individual relationship to water, to find pleasure and to make real progress in swimming, and not to think simply in terms of speed. It indicates a direction both for improving our stroke and discovering new avenues to explore how water can be enjoyed. More broadly, it provides a path for personal growth and empowerment. Swimming thus becomes more than a pleasurable and beneficial pastime. As the *art* of swimming, it can enhance our lives by providing a way of engaging in mindful and creative activity, and help to bring about a renewed sense of physical and emotional well-being.

THE ALEXANDER TECHNIQUE DEFINED

What is the Alexander Technique? Although it is becoming more widely known and practised, its essence is often misunderstood. It's not a form of relaxation treatment, massage, or a set of exercises designed to correct bad posture – although it is often used to reduce stress and improve poise. The Technique is primarily a method for teaching us to develop conscious control over a particular set of reactions, which are seen as the source of unproductive habits. The fundamental tendency is to *pull the head back and down*, either in response to an unpleasant stimulus, or simply because the movement has become an unconscious habit. The effect of this movement is to set in train a series of involuntary and unhelpful patterns of behaviour. Automatic physical reactions, with potentially negative effects on both mind and body, are not normally under our conscious control. They are habits into which we fall without thinking, unwittingly developed as a result of pressures imposed on us from infancy. They develop into a tendency to react to situations in ways over which we exercise limited conscious choice.

The Alexander Technique (abbreviated in this book to 'the Technique' or 'the AT') teaches us to re-assert effective command over the way we think and act. It starts by making us aware of how a balanced relationship between the head and back can have an important influence on the body as a whole. It gives us a means of intervening to inhibit the actions that disturb this balance, and so provides a foundation for us to prevent the unhelpful patterns which arise in consequence. It has been described as '*un*learning the habits of a lifetime', habits which perpetuate an unhealthy fragmentation of the self. We invariably go wrong when we divorce our mental processes from our physical being. The AT is a practical method for putting us back in touch with our bodies, and thereby bringing about a psycho - physical re-integration, which is particularly helpful in overcoming habits that impede the development of new skills. These principles are applicable to diverse activities in daily life: the AT is used in areas ranging from acting, riding, and golf to learning to play musical instruments and giving birth. The beneficial effects of the AT are widely recognised, and it is recommended by doctors and physical therapists as a method of alleviating a range of common ailments from stress to back pain.

Not only are unconscious habits an obstacle to mastering any creative activity, but they get in the way of enjoying the experience to the full. This is as true for swimming as for any other activity. Swimming can easily become boring if you plough through the water automatically, without any sense of development and exploration. Incorporating the AT brings the whole process to life. By opening ourselves to greater awareness through practising the Technique, we can discover in swimming a tremendous opportunity for continuing development and endless self-exploration. While AT phraseology sometimes reflects the Victorian era in which the Technique originated, the principles of the Technique have enduring and far-reaching implications for the art of swimming. The following sections give an account of how the AT developed and how it is taught today, introducing some of its main concepts in **bold print**.

Opposite: *Fig. 1.4   F. M. Alexander demonstrating the workings of his Technique*

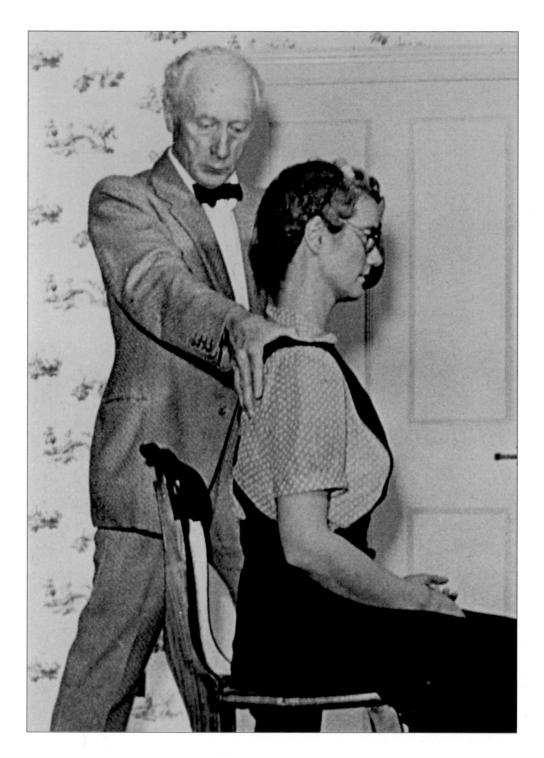

HOW THE ALEXANDER TECHNIQUE DEVELOPED

The story of how the Alexander Technique developed is worth telling both for its intrinsic interest and for the light it sheds on how it is practised today. Frederick Matthias Alexander, after whom the Technique is named, was born in Tasmania in 1869. He grew up in the an environment which offered him a wealth of opportunity to observe nature. A youthful interest in animals helped him to develop a keen sensitivity to the way both animals and humans move and function. In his early twenties he moved to Sydney with a view to becoming an actor. In the 1890s there was a vogue for the performance of dramatic recitations, in which actors would declaim on stage passages from Shakespeare and other dramatists. Although he was reasonably successful as a stage performer, Alexander was dismayed to find that his vocal chords seemed to seize up during performances so that he became hoarse or even lost his voice altogether. He sought medical treatment, but despite following a course of rest and medication he continued to experience a loss of vocal control when he returned to the stage.

Although he had suffered respiratory problems from birth, Alexander was forced to realise that his vocal difficulties were not caused by a condition which could be treated by conventional medical means. They were a direct consequence of his reaction to the strain of performing. In his view, something he was *doing to himself* – a physiological response to the conditions of performance – was causing him to lose his voice. To discover what was happening, he decided to find a way of observing himself while reciting. Using a structure of mirrors, he examined himself closely from different angles as he recreated the conditions of performing on stage. Over a long period of repeated self-observation he identified a particular movement which he invariably made as an involuntary reaction to stress: pulling his head *backwards and down*. The effect of this habitual action, he noted, was to alter the whole poise of his body, causing it to contract and stiffen. He gradually became convinced that this was the root of his problems. Among other things, it put severe pressure on his vocal mechanism, affecting his ability to breathe freely and to declaim.

Alexander subsequently became aware that the same reaction occurs in a wide variety of everyday activities, resulting in a degree of unnecessary tension in circumstances widely different from the stage. Pulling the head back and down is familiar as a defensive response in mammals, known as the **startle pattern**. It commonly occurs in the context of sudden fear or discomfort, the sort of conditions under which animals – and human beings – become immobilized or 'freeze' (*Fig. 1.5b*). Whatever its evolutionary purpose, it serves no useful function in everyday life. On the contrary, it tends to interfere with regular, effective functioning. The tension it creates throughout the body reflects the effort of combating the alarm which triggers it. Retracting our head in this way becomes so habitual that we rarely notice when it happens. Alexander concluded that the solution to his difficulties lay in teaching himself to become aware of this reaction and consciously to intervene to stop it happening. He set out to discover how, with the right kind of preparation, he might find a way of deliberately refusing to allow himself to react to stimuli in an automatic way. His new approach centred on becoming more aware of the relationship and balance between his head, neck and back. He came to regard this relationship as fundamental to his method, and for this reason termed it **the primary control**.

Fig. 1.5a   Neck free   Fig. 1.5b   Startle pattern

Although Alexander felt he had made an important discovery, the solution was not straightforward. He found that he constantly slipped back into habitual patterns without realising what was happening. Any attempt to reverse this by deliberately straightening up merely compounded his tension. He realised that it was important to eliminate any ill-conceived effort to 'correct' his posture. The solution was not to be sought in purely physical terms – by using the muscles in a one-off corrective measure – but involved both mind and body acting continuously together. Observing the processes that caused the distortion of his poise, he devised a system for combining mental and physical responses in an integrated way. As he learned to prevent patterns of what he called **misuse**, his voice problems receded. He also noticed a considerable improvement in his general health, including the disappearance of the breathing problems from which he had suffered since childhood. Resuming his acting career, he proceeded to apply his newly-acquired skills to improving his stage performances. Alexander described how his method evolved in his book *The Use of the Self*, and the concepts of **use** and **misuse** were to become central in the Technique.

Alexander had originally set out to find a solution to his own problems, but he became aware of the same patterns of misuse in nearly everyone he encountered. He initially began to teach his Technique as a method for overcoming breathing problems. He gradually developed his characteristic teaching system, a combination of verbal guidance and gentle **direction** with his hands, which aimed to foster in his pupils a new sensitivity stemming from a better, freer **head-neck-back relationship**. Shortly after the turn of the century he moved to London, where he continued to develop and teach his Technique until his death in 1955. Through his methods, many individuals have learned to discover their own patterns of psychophysical misuse and to overcome them by bringing them under **conscious control**. The Alexander Technique not only provides important insights into how to enhance health, but may be thought of as a method for getting in closer touch with ourselves. As such it has wider implications – akin to the philosophies of Zen and Yoga – as Alexander and other adherents of his method, such as authors George Bernard Shaw and Aldous Huxley, were quick to realise.

THE ALEXANDER TECHNIQUE IN PRACTICE

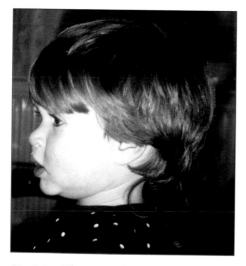

Fig. 1.6   The poise of a two-year old

When an investigation comes to be made, it will be found that the very thing we are doing in the work is exactly what is being done in nature where the conditions are right – the difference being that we are learning to do it consciously.

F. M. Alexander

As babies and young children we possess a natural poise which enables us to move without undue strain or effort (*Fig. 1.6*). As we grow older we acquire greater muscular control of our limbs, but in the process we lose a degree of flexibility. Children are regularly told to 'stand up straight', 'walk properly', 'sit still'. In striving to comply, it's no wonder that we acquire ways of using ourselves which interfere with natural ease of movement. Even in apparently simple activities like sitting and standing we use redundant movements and unnecessary

Fig. 1.7

*Teaching the Alexander Technique:
improving the awareness of our performance*

effort. Excessive tension accumulates and leads to physical strain, which can eventually result in specific symptoms such as headaches, sore backs, and frozen shoulders and necks. More generally, the strain shows itself in adults as stress, stiffness, and a lack of vitality and poise.

The Alexander Technique in practice tackles the source of these problems rather than the symptoms. Individual lessons are the norm. The teacher uses verbal suggestions and manual guidance to heighten awareness of misuse: for instance, directing the pupil by gentle pressure of the hands to sit down or rise from a chair, to walk around the room, or to lie on a table while the teacher's hands impart a sense of **lengthening and widening** throughout the body. A deeper understanding of the Technique and its effects tends to emerge in the course of lessons rather than being explicitly taught. Through prompting of hand and voice, the teacher encourages the **release** of over-tensed muscles and helps to reactivate natural reflexes (*Fig. 1.7*). These promote a sense of the upward **orientation** of the spine, allowing an overall release of the musculo-skeletal structure, more relaxed and fuller breathing, and freer movement of the limbs.

Teaching the AT differs from most types of teaching in that there is no 'right way' of doing it. The emphasis is actually taken away from trying to do the 'right' thing, and instead attention is directed towards *eliminating the wrong*. When it comes to the workings of our own bodies, our senses are surprisingly unreliable. We generally have inaccurate ideas about exactly what we do when we respond to stimuli such as a touch or a verbal instruction. F. M. Alexander called this **faulty** (or **unreliable**) **sensory appreciation**. It arises from unawareness of how we use our bodies, and is compounded by the dulling effects of years of habitual misuse. It is therefore important in learning the AT to understand that we cannot rely exclusively on sensation. All we can do is to remain open to the possibility of change.

While a trained eye can spot what happens when we react in our habitual fashion, our own senses are liable to give inaccurate information about what we are actually doing. Long-standing habits are so deeply ingrained that they have come to feel normal, and any change, even for the better, may initially feel wrong. Furthermore, when we actively *try* to bring about desired changes, we are almost certain to make matters worse. The inclination to try hard to achieve a given goal is, more often than not, a major obstacle to progress in learning.

F. M. Alexander frequently cautioned against this attitude, which he called **end-gaining**. Instead of focussing narrowly and unproductively on the ultimate goal of any activity, we are encouraged instead to be aware from moment to moment. This allows us to pay constructive attention to the actual experience and the specific processes involved in any action: in Alexander's term, to the **means-whereby**.

The *AT* emphasises that the muscles and frame of a living, breathing person are in a condition of dynamic balance, constantly on the move. For this reason, *AT* teachers *avoid* the word 'posture', which tends to imply a static pose – the sort of misuse familiar from images of soldiers on parade standing stiffly to attention (*Fig. 1.8*). The dynamic and mindful nature of the *AT* is brought out by its description as **thinking in activity**. Specific conditions, such as poor posture, back pain, or breathing difficulties, are viewed from the overall perspective of misuse. As described above, misuse most often occurs in connection with pulling the head back and down, as in the **startle reflex**. This action has a detrimental effect on overall functioning and leads to the build-up of strain. In the course of lessons in the *AT*, the pupil gradually learns to be aware of this reaction and to consciously prevent or **inhibit** it, promoting improvements in overall health and in the performance of everyday activities. Alexander's use of the term inhibition to refer to forestalling the habits which interfere with good use should be distinguished from the more common use of 'inhibition' nowadays to refer to the the suppression of painful emotions.

People who come to the *AT* suffering from specific ailments are often surprised that their problem is not focussed on directly. This is because modern medicine tends to treat different parts of our bodies in isolation, and the highly specialised medical approach does not encourage individuals to view themselves and their health in an integrated way. The *AT* by contrast is characterised by a holistic and non-direct approach to medical conditions. During lessons, attention is paid not to parts of the body in isolation but to the co-ordination and balance of the *whole* organism. The experience of *AT* students, as of Alexander himself, is that remarkable and sustained improvements in specific conditions can be made through bringing about the improved functioning of the organism as a whole.

Fig. 1.8

'Atten-SHUN!'

THINKING IN ACTIVITY

The Alexander Technique opens a window onto the little known area
between stimulus and response and gives you the self-knowledge
you need in order to change the pattern of your response.
Frank Pierce Jones

The initial lesson in learning the *AT* is to become aware of our habitual reactions and to apply the decision to *stop*. Once we have learned to prevent an unthinking reaction we can choose to apply a response based on reasoned judgement. Responding in this way requires us to attend to ourselves in the present moment. Stopping unthinking habits puts us in the position of being able to exercise choice rather than be subservient to unchecked automatic reactions. The radical difference between our normal patterns of behaviour and the process of **thinking in activity** can be illustrated by the following model (*Fig. 1.9*). In this model we see how one pathway leads to a pattern of habitual reactions which result in a 'vicious spiral' of misuse, tension and pain. Conversely, by learning to break the habit, we enter into a 'virtuous spiral' of awareness and the freedom to act in a healthy way.

Fig. 1.9

PATHWAY 1 Stimulus –
Non-thinking response ➤ Tension ➤ Misuse ➤ Pain ➤ Non-thinking response

PATHWAY 2 Stimulus – Awareness ➤ Release ➤ Poise ➤ Ease ➤ Awareness

---

It's not easy to remain constantly alert to ourselves in this way. We are creatures of habit, and not used to the idea that we can renew our self-awareness from second to second. Inevitably, we find ourselves slipping back into habitual reactions and unthinking habits. However, through practice of the *AT* it becomes easier to notice the signals of misuse and to respond in an appropriate way.

Alexander frequently said that only by *stopping the wrong* can better use emerge, and in the *AT* great importance is attached to this principle. As the pupil progresses, understanding of what 'stopping' entails matures and deepens. It doesn't mean doing nothing at all so that you collapse in a heap. It relates specifically to stopping the familiar, unwanted and unnecessary habits of our physical and mental responses. Only in this way can we recognise how habitual these patterns are, and be empowered to overcome them so that we can live our lives with a new and more creative awareness.

THE FORCE OF HABIT

When he comes into my room at first, I ask him to sit down as a
matter of etiquette – and when he sits down in that chair,
I have a history of his life's use of himself.
F.M. Alexander

Everything we do involves a complex interaction of conscious and unconscious actions. As we have shown, in practice the *AT* tends to work with relatively undemanding, commonplace activities, like standing, sitting, and walking. The effort of performing more complicated activities is likely to furnish distractions from the initial task at hand, that of learning to be aware of ourselves. Krishna-murti once remarked 'There is more to life than getting in and out of a chair!' Equally, one could say that there is more to playing the piano than just pressing the keys; but to be able to do so with the appropriate amount of weight and balance is the foundation of all further learning of the instrument. In the same way, even sitting and standing with a new mindfulness can bring enormous benefit. It is the basis of a self-awareness that can be extended to all activities.

Are you aware which sets of muscles you use when you get up from a chair? Logically, you may agree, the most efficient way of doing this would be to let your lower body – legs, hips and lower back – do most, if not all, of the work. But notice for yourself what happens when you begin to stand up. Do you find your neck or shoulders tensing? Are muscles in your upper body contracting?

The decision to rise from a chair is often accompanied by a contraction of neck muscles which pulls the head back. This is followed by an unnecessary downward pressure on the legs. These responses are so habitual that we don't notice ourselves making them. But are they necessary or desirable? The small backward movement of the head, part of the 'startle pattern' mentioned above, creates a strain on the neck and a contraction of the spine. Put simply, we are *doing too much*. Note the lightness and grace of a cat jumping up onto a wall, or a monkey springing from a branch (*Fig. 1.10*): because it is oriented upwards, it exerts the minimum necessary downward force. Its head and body function as an integrated unit. Similarly, what is needed for you to rise from your chair is for your body to be well oriented in an upward direction. All the relevant muscles are then engaged at the right moment, working together in harmony to take your body upwards.

Fig. 1.10   *Exhibiting perfect balance, a monkey leaps across a wide gap with ease*

In this way, even getting out of a chair requires a lot less effort than we normally use.

When we get up or sit down in our habitual, unthinking manner, the unnecessary muscular tension that we have engaged in our body and limbs persists. Our muscles stay taut, our spine remains contracted. Our body becomes effectively locked in a state of unnecessary strain, which in turn affects our thinking (the 'vicious spiral' of Fig. 1.9) In subsequent actions – walking, driving, climbing stairs – we labour under the disadvantage of already lacking the basis for dynamic poise and flexibility. The constant repetition of such actions in the course of a day compounds the strain we unwittingly place on our musculo-skeletal structure, sapping us of freshness and vitality. The cumulative effects of misuse thus affect both bodily and mental functioning. No wonder most people feel drained at the end of a working day.

By proposing that we direct attention to the starting-point of the tension at the top of the spine (known as the atlanto-occipital or 'nodding' joint) – the AT proposes a practical way in which we can become, and remain, alert to ourselves. In the AT session, divorced from distractions, our mind is sufficiently quiet to be aware of what we are doing when we start to rise from a chair. In our habitual mode this is likely to involve a host of extraneous, unhelpful movements and tensions – pulling back our head, hollowing our back, tensing our shoulders and so on. So the first thing we're encouraged to do is to stop doing what we usually do. By consciously forestalling our habitual reaction, we can allow the relationship of our head and back to remain balanced and flexible. We remain in a condition of **release**, in which we are poised to choose how to engage ourselves most efficiently to achieve the desired result. The outcome is the continuous positive cycle, reinforcing both physical and psychological ease (*Fig. 1.9*).

What emerges from this account is that the *AT* is first and foremost about *breaking the force of habit*. It is not intended as a method for replacing bad habits with good ones. Inasmuch as habits are unthinking, the *AT* shuns them altogether. In the words of the philosopher William James, who had a high regard for Alexander's work, 'The only habit to cultivate is the habit of giving up habits'. True awareness is thinking in the moment and not relying on habit. Only in this way can we approach any situation with a fresh and open mind. Greater awareness of our use brings with it the challenge of exploration and genuine discovery.

AWARENESS IN THE WATER

How can this sense of discovery be applied to swimming? Most swimmers are locked into unthinking patterns of behaviour in the water. These range from swimming with the head pulled back regardless of the strain and pain it produces, to ploughing through the water for long periods in a mindless fashion. Such patterns often stem from fears or persistent misapprehensions which have never been properly articulated or questioned. They serve as a block to achieving a sense of true freedom in the water, and lead to feelings of boredom and apathy about swimming. Tackling these patterns at their root releases a spirit of exploration which enlivens the whole process of swimming. Every stroke becomes an opportunity for discovery and self-exploration, expanding our horizon and opening up a new realm of possibility. Recognising the consistent interconnection between mental and physical habits, and becoming aware of mindless patterns, are the first steps towards acquiring the ability to approach the water without anxiety or strain.

Traditional swimming-teaching underestimates the way the force of habit gets in the way of learning. The assumption is that if learners are told or shown how to do something, they will be able to do it. The problem is that habits dictate our whole pattern of action. Although they can sometimes offer a short cut to building up our skills, they can also impede the optimum development of those skills. Once they have become fixed, they can be very hard to dislodge. These habits of both thought and action are observable in swimmers at all levels.

Whether it's the beginner pulling back his head in response to water splashing in his face, or the Olympic swimmer developing an unexpected stroke fault in her effort to win a race, their problems can be traced to an inability to overcome their unthinking habit.

Most swimming environments are likely to present greater distractions than an AT teaching room. On top of external distractions, swimmers have to contend with private anxieties about being lightly-clad, getting wet, submerging their face in water, swimming in public, and numerous other more-or-less unexpressed concerns. It's quite a challenge to retain one's awareness under such conditions. Anxiety often has the apparent effect of heightening awareness because it intensifies certain sensations. You will have noticed how under intimidating conditions lights can seem brighter, distances larger, and noises louder. In fact, these very perceptions shift your awareness away from your self and your relationship to the immediate surroundings. What is required under these circumstances is to quieten your mind. The AT encourages this by directing attention, in the first instance, to the most fundamental aspect of use – the relationship between head, neck and back (the **primary control**).

The other side of the coin is that water can be an extremely liberating, reflective, and sensual medium for exploration. It has exciting and unusual properties. For instance, buoyancy allows us to get as close to weightlessness as we are likely to experience short of travelling in space. Liquidity offers the possibility of uniquely pleasurable sensations. It is well known that being submerged in water has calming and uplifting effects. Water challenges us to discover how to use our whole body to manoeuvre through it successfully. It magnifies the effects of good and bad use. For example, the effect of pulling the head backwards and down can be more noticeable in the water than outside: it causes the lower body to sink down, creating greater resistance to our attempts at propulsion. Factors of this kind can waken in us a greater awareness of our immediate experience.

Even when we are sufficiently used to our surroundings for them not to be unduly distracting, another familiar habitual tendency comes into play: the desire to make active efforts to achieve our ends. This is related to the whole issue of end-gaining outlined above, and will be discussed in greater detail in a later chapter. At this stage it should be reiterated that the first steps to awareness involve precisely the opposite of making active efforts. Before any benefit can arise, first you have to stop and do nothing. Just by dropping the habit of being more active than you need, you allow yourself to remain constantly aware of your habitual reactions and your use.

This applies to each and every stage of your approach to the water: the efforts you make when changing into swim-wear, when walking to the pool, when getting into the water, when submerging your face, when performing a stroke. When it comes to acquiring new skills, swimmers of all levels are inclined to apply excessive effort. But as the Case Studies in this chapter show, even (in fact, especially) the first step in swimming – learning to float – is not something you actually *do*. Trying to hold ourselves up in the water has exactly the opposite effect to what is intended. What we must learn is to let go and allow the water to support the body. Being constantly on guard and learning to stop is the way to unlearn the habit of doing too much. As the unnecessary obstacles posed by our efforts are stripped away, a virtuous cycle arises in which natural and effective water skills are allowed to emerge and flourish (*Fig 1.11*). These bring about the quiet confidence that allows us to maintain our awareness and enjoy the experience of being in the water.

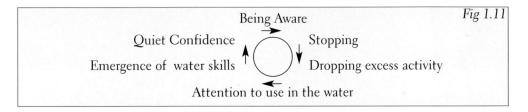

Fig 1.11

Being Aware

Quiet Confidence   Stopping

Emergence of water skills   Dropping excess activity

Attention to use in the water

Case Study 1A: *Ruth – Learning the Breast Stroke*

Ruth enjoyed swimming but encountered the common problem of being unable to co-ordinate the breaststroke in a satisfactory way. However rapidly she moved her arms and legs, she could not make steady progress through the water. She found the experience difficult and tiring, taking up to fifteen strokes to swim across the width of the pool. A former dancer, she was puzzled that her problems with co-ordination were exclusive to the water, and sought instruction to help her with her difficulties.

Her belief that she needed to learn to move the right way was only half the story. When she practised the stroke under supervision, she was shown how the immediate effect of action by the arms and legs was to make the body slow down. She became aware how, each time she pulled up her knees, her body momentarily stopped gliding steadily through the water. It became clear that the only time she actually moved for any length of time through the water was after her powerful leg-kick, when simply doing nothing allowed her body to glide forward, relaxed and fully extended. By taking full advantage of this, she discovered that the new orientation of her body allowed her more time to think and explore the optimum co-ordination of her arms and legs. She soon found herself crossing the width easily with a few kicks.

PRIMARY CONTROL IN THE WATER

A central concept of the *AT* is the primary control – the relationship between the head, neck and back in governing the overall use and functioning of the body. The relation of the head to the rest of the body is crucial to establishing poise and freedom of movement, because of its effect on the contraction and extension of the spinal column, the muscles of the neck and upper body – and through these on the rib-cage, breathing apparatus, and our whole musculo-skeletal structure. This relationship is truly dynamic: virtually every movement we make involves a change in it. At the heart of the *AT* is the concept that we can replace unconscious alterations to this balance, which work to our detriment, with conscious adjustments that work in favour of helping us to function efficiently. The habitual response of pulling the head backwards and down is prevented by conscious decision. In its place, at every opportunity, we can discover a more natural and healthy response which allows for lengthening and widening throughout the body.

In the water, even a small re-alignment of the head and neck can have a dramatic effect on the balance and orientation of the body. Because of the body's horizontal position, the head acts as an important counterweight and agent of balance. In particular, when the head is pulled back in the prone (face-down)

Fig. 1.12   *Moving the head forward and up brings the hips back and down*

strokes, it alters the balance of the whole body so that the hips begin to sink. When swimming on our backs, the same result is achieved by bringing the head forward and up (*Fig. 1.12*).

Swimmers who concentrate on propulsion through the water commonly focus on their arms and legs, paying insufficient attention to the use of the whole body. As a result, the majority of swimmers have little awareness of how their head is moving relative to the rest of their body when they swim. Many swimming manuals lay stress on 'body position' as an important aspect of swimming technique. However, this can imply an over-rigid positioning of one's head relative to the rest of the body, which militates against good use in the water. It's not body *position*, but a **forward-and-upward** *direction* and a dynamic balance of one's whole physical structure that are all-important. The importance of the primary control for bringing this about will be explored in a later chapter, *Leading with the Head: Orientation & Balance*.

Case Study 1B: *Oliver – Learning to Float*

At 30, Oliver was convinced that he had a fundamental problem with water. Tall, heavy-boned and muscular, he contended that he was simply unable to float. He imagined himself as a solid pole which sank in the water like a stone. As a result, he would not get into the water without creating a great deal of movement with his arms and legs in order to try to keep himself afloat. He resolutely kept his head above the water surface to ensure that he could breathe. The result was that he would rapidly become tired and breathless. The rigid position of his head above the water added to the natural tendency of his hips to sink under the weight of his long legs, leading to discomfort and neck-strain after just a short time in the water.

He was dubious when told that he would only float if he did less to prevent it. Although he understood that the air in the body and lungs could provide buoyancy for the whole body, he had never experienced floating, since he had never lain still in the water and allowed his torso to lengthen and widen. He was first persuaded to release his head down into the water, so that the new orientation of his upper body might allow his chest and lungs to act as a natural buoy. Although he initially sank below the surface, he found that when he did nothing his upper body eventually floated upwards, allowing him to breathe simply by lifting his head. After a few lessons of just gliding without moving his arms and legs, he became aware of how he had been locking the well-developed muscles of his torso in his efforts to hold himself up in the water. The less he actually tried to do, the more he could allow his upper body to assert its natural buoyancy.

CONCLUSION

A man is but the product of his thoughts:
what he thinks, he becomes.
Mahatma Gandhi

This chapter has introduced the range of different concepts used in the Alexander Technique: the unity of the self, psychophysical awareness, habit and inhibition, the unreliability of sensation, use and misuse, and the primary control. It has outlined how these concepts can be applied and developed in the water, to establish a basis for effective swimming and to enhance the quality of the experience. While the emphasis of the AT in practice can appear to be on purely physical aspects of activity, the intimate connection of mental and physical is considered to be present at every level of action. Creating a more balanced head-neck-back relationship helps us to *think* more freely about our use, while increased attention to use brings about greater *physical* ease. In practising the AT, cause and effect are linked in a circular process of continuous positive feedback.

The mental space created by increased physical ease allows us to expand our attention and explore our *self* constructively in all types and aspects of activity. The development of awareness through the AT is invaluable as a preparation for changing our patterns of behaviour and developing new skills. Because of the unique and unusual properties of water, the specific application of the AT to an aquatic environment opens up new possibilities for experience and exploration. Systems of philosophy concur that we only experience life to the full when we live totally in the present. Not only does practice of the Technique offer indications about how we might think constructively about swimming, but the lessons of awareness in the water expand our potential to understand the way we use ourselves from moment to moment outside the water.

The remainder of this book looks in detail at the aspects of the AT outlined in this chapter, and explores how they can be effectively integrated with the key elements of swimming. In the course of our exploration it should become clear how both the AT and the art of swimming have a wider significance than might at first be imagined. Both invite philosophical reflections that are grounded in human experience: ideas of change, flow, balance and harmony. Together they open up a new vista of possibilities for growth and self-development.

chapter two

at home in the water

'I'm very brave generally', he went on in a low voice:
'only today I happen to have a headache'.
Lewis Carroll

The only thing we have to fear is fear itself.
Franklin D. Roosevelt

What comes to mind when we see someone swimming with ease and grace?
'A fish in the water', 'water-baby', 'natural swimmer' – these are the sort of terms
we use. What separates such swimmers from those who are merely competent is
clearly not just style or technique. They give the impression that there are no
psychological barriers preventing them from interacting with the water in a complete and satisfying way. By contrast, one of the main obstacles in learning the
art of swimming is the uncertainty that is so often felt about relating to the water.
This ranges from persistent mild unease to attacks of sudden panic. The former
constrains our freedom to explore the aquatic environment, and the latter can
be as debilitating as full-scale aquaphobia. At either end of the spectrum, the
thought of being surrounded by an alien medium results in feelings of psychological and physical discomfort. One can know how to swim, and even consider
oneself a good swimmer, without feeling completely *at home* in the water.

Being at home in the water is a matter of trust. Trust in the water's ability to
support the body without the need for us to hold ourselves up. Trust in our own
ability to manoeuvre efficiently in a fluid medium. This trust comes about
through understanding and familiarity. It needs to be cultivated and positively
reinforced by our experience with water. Yet unfortunately our confidence is
often undermined by attitudes which we find hard to shake off. Recurring mis-
trust of the water and about our ability to negotiate it are self-fulfilling. But too
often, such anxieties are swept under the carpet. Teachers and guidebooks don't
deal adequately, if at all, with these issues. Swimmers themselves often trivialize
and even deny them in the belief that they are best dealt with by being mini-
mized or ignored. But the results of doing this can be far from trivial: it allows
unhelpful reactions and feelings to be reinforced, and risks creating a vicious

Fig. 2.1   *An environment of trust is crucial in learning to swim*

cycle of the kind we described in Chapter 1 (*Fig. 1.9, p. 26*). To avoid such a scenario, anxieties of all kinds relating to swimming should always be dealt with sympathetically and appreciated for what they are.

Fear of water is not the same as respect for water. Even the strongest of swimmers needs to have a healthy respect for water and an awareness of its hazards. Powerful tides and currents – and in some waters, marine animals like sharks and jellyfish – can mean real danger for swimmers who don't heed warnings or take sensible precautions. It's foolish to take unnecessary risks or to be insufficiently prepared in any aquatic situation. Intelligence dictates that we acknowledge our limitations *vis-à-vis* the water and always take appropriate safety measures. Whilst accidents can occur as a result of misplaced over-confidence, fear itself is often the main factor that prevents us making an intelligent response. Fear can paralyse us both mentally and physically. It interferes with our breathing and our ability to control our movements, and stops us thinking clearly enough to manoeuvre our way out of danger. Over the longer term too, the dulling nature of unresolved anxieties and the cumulative effects of fear get in the way of intelligent learning and a creative response to our immediate situation.

OUR EARLY EXPERIENCE OF WATER

Child of Nature, learn to unlearn.
Benjamin Disraeli

New-born babies have a natural affinity with water. We pass the first nine months or so after conception in a safe, controlled environment, entirely surrounded by water. As we float in the womb, our prenatal experiences are pleasurable sensations of support, comfort and warmth. Familiarity with the medium gives babies a natural sense of being at home in the water – water-births are an increasingly popular option. The ability to negotiate water without fear extends into the first few months of infancy. The ability to swim is considered to be a primitive reflex. Just as an infant will have an automatic reaction to curl its hand around small objects (the grasping reflex), so a baby immersed in water will automatically move its limbs and stop breathing in, so as to stay afloat and prevent water entering its lungs. The swimming reflex gradually disappears during the first year of life.

When we observe small infants at bathtime we see how the water rarely presents a threat. As long as they feel secure and supported, it's a comfortable and pleasurable experience for them (*Fig. 2.2*). Infant swimming classes are designed to build on this natural confidence before fears have an opportunity to set in. However, it's questionable whether formal swimming lessons at the infant stage are useful or desirable. The danger is that both child and parent may acquire a false confidence in the infant's ability to cope with the environment of water. It's inappropriate to expect very young children to be sufficiently safety-conscious on their own, and they should only be allowed to play and have fun in water under adult supervision.

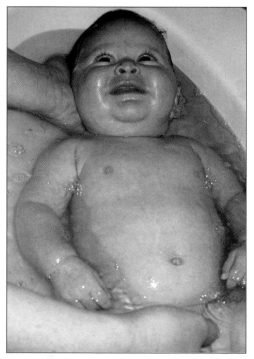

Fig. 2.2 Babies feel at home in the water

Fig. 2.3   *An infant shows confidence and natural poise under the water.*

The swimming reflex shows suggests human beings have a certain innate ability to stay afloat and to move through the water. However, this can be and is often quickly *un*learned. Our attitude to the water is largely shaped during the psychologically critical period of our early years. Unfortunately, what is learned at this early stage is fear. This above all changes the quality of children's experience to one in which they no longer feel at home in the water. For most children, the early confidence about water is soon forgotten.

How does fear arise? The most common reason is that the child unconsciously notices and internalizes the fears exhibited by parents or primary carers. When such individuals show anxiety about being in the water themselves, or make obvious their concern that the child is in danger, they transmit their apprehensions to the child. The opposite is the case if a feeling of confidence and pleasure is transmitted (*Fig. 2.4*). Young children can be profoundly sensitive to such feelings when projected by a parent or a significant person in their environment. In particular, the latters' sense of not being at home in water is forcefully communicated. Other factors add to the overriding psychological impact of this message. For example, the infant may recoil from the discomfort of being cold and wet. But this need not develop into fear of water unless the experience is associated with an unhappy sense of insecurity.

Many adults who express anxiety about swimming relate their fears to negative childhood experiences of the water, in particular occasions when they felt that they were in danger of drowning. Such experiences can be so traumatic that they produce phobic reactions to water which can be very hard to overcome. They can result in the unreasonable conviction 'I can't swim' – and more insidiously, in the excuse 'I don't *want* to learn to swim because I don't like water'. Not everyone, of course, has such an extreme reaction. Many people manage to swim despite their fears, but remarkably often a residual awkwardness or tension is apparent. We nearly all remain influenced by early experiences which act as a block to our progress in the water. Once we learn to appreciate their limiting effects, we can realise that a much fuller enjoyment of swimming may be gained by changing our whole approach to the water.

Fig. 2.4   *Support inspires confidence*

THE LEARNING OF FEAR

Most learning is not the result of instruction. It is rather the result
of unhampered participation in a meaningful setting.
Ivan Illich

Fear is all around us. We go through life being afraid – of people, events, death, the unknown, ourselves, and of fear itself. One effect of fear is that it stops us reaching our full potential, by getting in the way of our acquiring new knowledge and skills. This can result from those around us, even if they mean well, themselves being afraid of our growing, changing, and discovering our potential as individuals. Their fear on our behalf reflects their own fear of change. Life, however, is a constant process of change. While change can make us feel vulnerable, the alternative to embracing it is to live in a narrower world, surrounded by walls of fear and uncertainty. As this image suggests, by attempting to reject change we become restricted both in our bodies and our thinking. Fear disempowers us, making discovery of the *new* less appealing than repetition of the *known*. Whilst we may thus acquire a superficial sense of security, ultimately it leads to further insecurity – the consequence of stagnation and inflexibility. It stops us from thinking creatively, both in what we're doing and about how we want to experience our lives. We restrict ourselves through fear of humiliation, ignorance, solitude, society, pain, disease, or dying. And confusingly, sometimes through fear of growth, success, freedom – even love. At least we need to understand more clearly what we're afraid of if we wish to overcome the fear and move forward.

Systems of education and social and parental pressures insidiously encourage the development of fear. Trying to do something 'right' – that is, in a way pleasing to those in authority – is the flip side of the fear of making mistakes. F. M. Alexander noted 'If you could stop the tremendous effort of trying to be right, you might actually be able to achieve your desired end!' Making mistakes is an inevitable and useful part of the learning process. When learning to speak a foreign language, if we're concerned with speaking it correctly all the time we are likely to remain tongue-tied. When you catch yourself doing something incorrectly, you shouldn't just be frustrated or annoyed with yourself – you should take credit for recognizing it. Even if criticism itself can be constructive, fear of criticism is likely to be unhelpful. To learn, we need to be able to accept advice in an open and uninhibited way. For this to be possible, we need to feel safe about making and noticing our mistakes. Children who are brought up in an environment where the response to making a mistake is ridicule or punishment are unlikely to allow themselves to think or act freely and creatively. A secure and supportive framework is essential for learning.

In dealing with fear, physical contact can be an important means of reassurance. Manual support and guidance is an effective teaching tool in swimming, but conventional teaching methods offer little constructive advice or training in such techniques. The usual environment for teaching swimming is one in which the teacher is an authority figure. Teachers and coaches have most commonly carried out swimming instruction standing outside the water, shouting orders to groups of pupils with whom they have limited or no physical contact. From a child's perspective, the coach towers above, teaching by command rather than by example. The teacher's apparent aloofness can seem unsupportive and intimidating. Children may also be swept along by competitive peer pressures, thereby missing out on valuable lessons of confidence and safety. Group dynamics can mean that individual children are forced to suppress their own fears and inadequacies so as not to be singled out.

Much depends on the teacher's own skill and perceptiveness. There is no doubt that in many circumstances group teaching can be effective, as well as time-saving and cost-efficient. However, responsible one-to-one physical assistance in the water may be invaluable in imparting a feeling of confidence and safety both to children and adult learners. Traditional methods of swimming-teaching do not provide instructors with the rationale or explicit techniques for giving pupils constructive physical support in the water. Concerns about abuse of children in particular has led to a climate in which swimming-teachers are discouraged from any kind of physical contact with young pupils. In teaching the *AT* (in or out of the water) the primary emphasis is on the head-neck-back relationship, and the use of the teacher's hands for guidance in this area means that swimming instruction with the *AT* is hands-on as well. The formulation of explicit guidelines on touch makes both teachers and pupils more aware of appropriate boundaries.

All teachers agree that a sense of confidence in water is essential to swimming. However, insufficient attention is paid to the specific issues that must be addressed if the learner is to acquire confidence. This neglect partly stems from thinking of swimming as a purely physical activity. It's assumed that the development of

Fig. 2.5   Poor teaching inspires fear rather than confidence

swimming skills alone is enough for the learner to become confident about the water. This is rarely the case. When skills are acquired without first establishing a sound basis of confidence, a crucial aspect of swimming is bypassed. This omission is at the expense of a whole dimension of sensitivity to being in the water and a more profound enjoyment of swimming. The situation may be illustrated by the following model:

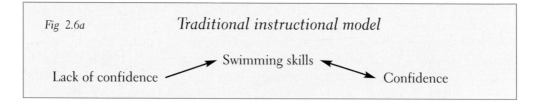

Fig 2.6a   *Traditional instructional model*

It's true that acquiring competent motor skills leads to greater confidence in water, which in turn encourages the further development of such skills. The better you're able to move through water, the more confident you're bound to feel about being in the water. But your confidence will not be well grounded if it is treated merely as a by-product of skills, as the model illustrates. Supposing an unexpected situation arises – an attack of cramp or water splashing unexpectedly in your face. Well-practised motor skills can become inadequate or irrelevant. In the face of such an occurrence the left-hand arrow swings round, and the pathway leads straight back to the initial situation – inability and fear. The fact that your swimming skills are based on inadequate foundations means there is a sense of precariousness and unease about the whole question of being in the water.

Far better, then, that teaching should include explicit instruction to establish confidence, both prior to and parallel with the development of motor skills in the water. This requires a shift of emphasis. The revised instructional model shows a teaching path which leads *via* confidence-building measures to the development of soundly based swimming skills:

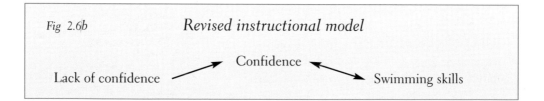

Fig 2.6b   *Revised instructional model*

This model is a useful basis for thinking about the learning of any skill. The educationist John Dewey saw the *AT* in a similar light, as being an essential preliminary to the acquisition of learning. He wrote that the *AT* 'bears the same relation to education that education bears to all other human activities'.

Fig. 2.7   *Forward and up*

TENSE MIND, TENSE BODY

What happens when we're afraid, anxious or shocked? Our whole body registers the response in a variety of ways. Fear is more than a purely psychological matter. In fact, it highlights the inseparability of the psychological and physiological domains. Expressions associated with fear include 'seizing up' and 'becoming rigid', a 'sinking feeling' or a 'knot in the stomach'. Such reactions exemplify the characteristic sense of discomfort associated with feeling afraid. They have physiological correlates in the disposition of our musculo-skeletal structure and the release of chemicals into our bloodstream. These changes are not under our conscious control. That's why the instruction 'Don't be afraid' can be asking a lot of someone undergoing the experience of real fear.

All mammals have similar physiological reactions to the experience of danger or to its perceived threat. In this situation, a series of chemical impulses is triggered in the autonomic nervous system, resulting in instantaneous changes in the body. These include changes in the cardiovascular system, as adrenalin is produced to facilitate a burst of energetic movement; changes in the respiratory system – breathing becomes shallower and more rapid; and a temporary shutdown of the digestive system, to allow more energy to be transferred to the limbs. These reactions are the body's way of preparing to negotiate danger by fighting, freezing or running away. The exact nature of the changes and the way in which they are felt vary between species and individuals. Human beings asso-

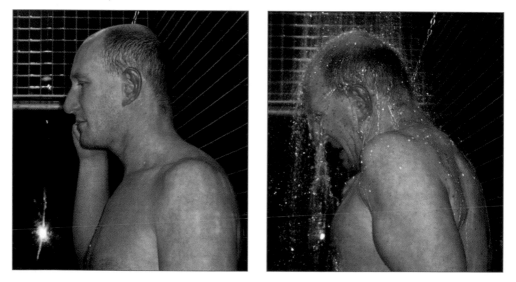

Fig. 2.7   *Cold water can have a startling effect*

ciate the experience with sensations such as a pounding heart, sweating, dryness of the mouth, and a tightening of the chest. The effects can be clearly seen when people receive a sudden shock. Their bodies stiffen, their eyes widen or close, and their faces change colour (*Fig. 2.7*).

The difference between the fear response in human beings and in other mammals is that for animals the effects are short-lived and usually pass as soon as danger recedes. In humans they endure, and sometimes persist long after the threat has passed. In the case of a particularly traumatic event, psychophysical symptoms can persist for several days, weeks or even years. It's as if the experience remains trapped in our bodies. People who are scared of swimming often recall a particular episode in their past when they felt an acute sense of fear of being in water. The experience can have such a marked effect that the mere thought of swimming makes them extremely nervous. These fear responses are so ingrained that aquaphobes convince themselves that they will never be able to shake off their fear.

However, there is at least one aspect of our fear reactions which, once we are made fully aware of it, we can learn to bring under our conscious control to some degree. This is the **startle pattern**, the operation of which is central to the Alexander Technique. When we receive a sudden shock – a loud noise or bright light in our faces, or an unexpected piece of bad news – we have a tendency to contract the muscles of our neck involuntarily, causing the head to be thrust backwards. Muscular reactions which accompany this response include raising our shoulders, tensing our arms, stiffening our chests, and flexing the leg muscles so that our knees lock. All this takes place within a split second. These reactions have evolved as an automatic defensive response in the face of danger, and therefore are extremely difficult, if not impossible, to avoid in most circumstances.

Although the most dramatic manifestations of the startle pattern can be observed at moments of extreme tension, less pronounced forms can be detected in everyday situations. At home or at work, in public or in private, we are subjected to situations and events which can cause us to seize up with worry or apprehension. It can even happen when the phone rings. However, we can learn to exercise some conscious control so that the impact of the startle pattern is reduced and its effects do not linger. By cultivating a more balanced and aware disposition through the AT, we can prevent it taking place as often as it might, and learn how to minimize its effects.

Some types of anxiety are so pronounced and incapacitating that they are considered serious psychological disorders, and are classified as phobias. These include fear of spiders, of being enclosed, or of public places. Aquaphobia, commonly used to mean fear of swimming, is rarely included in such classifications (hydrophobia, where water is avoided even for drinking, is a symptom of rabies).

Specific treatments have been devised to help reduce or eliminate phobias. For instance, cognitive therapies work on the premise that one first needs to examine and understand the irrational nature of one's fear in order to be released from it. Combined with behavioural techniques, such as gradual exposure to fear-inducing situations, they have proved particularly effective. An approach to the problem of 'mental blocks' was developed by Wilhelm Reich, a one-time student of Freud's. Reich believed that traumatic experiences remain fixed in our musculature. He identified the 'character-muscular armour' as the main obstacle to healthy psychological functioning. 'Character armour' consists of defensive character traits (such as debilitating shyness) developed in childhood as a way of warding off painful feelings. 'Muscular armour' is manifested in the muscular spasms which represent the bodily expression of these attitudes. Reich proposed a combination of psychotherapeutic and physical techniques to break down such emotional armouring and to release pent-up psychic and physical energies.

Fig. 2.8

This approach has certain similarities to that adopted by the *AT*. The Technique is less concerned with analysing the origins of fear than with learning to undo what Alexander called 'over-excited fear responses'. In practice, remembering an early traumatic event related to swimming does little to help the inhibition of extreme psychophysical reactions that occur in or near a swimming-pool. Dwelling on negative experiences in the past can even increase the feeling of fear associated with swimming. From the *AT* perspective, working directly with the fear *reactions* is the key to eradicating disabling symptoms of anxiety. This is achieved by first awakening a fuller awareness of the reactions themselves, and then showing how they can be mastered. Attention to the 'means-whereby' – the best use of oneself in the present moment – is a remarkably

Swimming is not about keeping the hair dry

46

Case Study 3:   *Amanda – Overcoming Aquaphobia*

At 40, Amanda was a self-confessed aquaphobe. The thought of having to swim was enough to make her tremble and come out in a cold sweat. This she attributed to an early experience when she was thrown into deep water by a (so-called) swimming instructor. She recalled the event with great clarity, remembering in detail how she had felt at the time. She thought she was going to drown, and was pulled from the pool in a state of abject terror.

With great courage, Amanda decided to try to overcome her phobia by confronting her fear head-on. She enrolled on a course of group swimming lessons, but after several months had made very little progress. Although she was able to enter a shallow pool and propel herself for a short distance, the sense of panic persisted. Around the same time, she embarked on a series of AT lessons to help her deal with a chronic back condition. She was referred to an AT swimming instructor, who adopted a one-to-one approach that was radically different from her previous teacher's. Amanda's attention was drawn to her habitual response of tensing her neck and holding her breath. The teacher supported her head and neck as she lay on her back in the water, and gently pulled her along, ensuring that she was breathing easily and that her neck muscles remained free. After a few lessons she was able to float unaided, and proceeded to learn to perform the various strokes. Her most important lesson was that of trust: she had learned to trust first her teacher, then the water, and ultimately herself.

effective way of removing an unproductive focus on the original source of anxiety. This involves a redirection of attention from the fear itself to the process involved in performing the activity (see the Case Study above). People who are afraid of water are rarely aware of their specific reactions to it. Armed with a new awareness of the obstacles they are creating for themselves, they can work effectively on letting go of the patterns of action into which they fall without thinking. In this way they can eventually discover for themselves that the water can be a safe, comfortable and enjoyable environment.

The practice of the Alexander Technique encourages a sense of continual exploration and self-discovery. Exploration requires the readiness to embrace the new in order to discover and experience the unknown. The AT challenges us to confront our fears by becoming aware of how habitual reactions limit us and prevent personal growth. The 'forward and up' of the AT is a movement that is both literal and symbolic. It represents leaving our fears behind and progressing to a higher level of thought and action in our daily lives.

FACING THE WATER WITH CONFIDENCE

Whoever looks into the mirror of the water will see first of all his own face.
Whoever goes to himself risks a confrontation with himself. The mirror
does not flatter, it faithfully shows whatever looks into it... This
confrontation is the first test of courage on the inner
way, a test sufficient to frighten off most people.

Carl Jung

Not many people are afraid of putting their feet in water. Or their hands. Or their hips, their arms, theirs shoulders, their necks...But if there is a sticking-point, it is invariably the face. What is it about the face that makes it seem so vulnerable? The short answer is – hair, eyes, nose, ears, and mouth! And particularly the nose. Sniffing water into the nostrils can be extremely unpleasant – a stinging, burning sensation. But it is not fatal, and despite all evidence to the contrary, many people behave as if simply submerging their face will subject its vital and sensitive orifices to intense discomfort or to the unstoppable influx of water. Is there any basis for such fears? Most swimmers would readily agree that such concerns are exaggerated. Nonetheless, whether or not rationally or even consciously held, they need to be thought about and addressed. They are obstacles to appreciating how the immersion of the face is a necessary, integral, and potentially greatly rewarding aspect of the art of swimming.

The eyes are undoubtedly delicate and sensitive organs. Most of us detest the sensation of medicinal drops being dripped into our eyes. When a foreign body touches the cornea, our automatic reaction is to blink and flicker our eyelids, and there's a natural tendency for the eye to water. These reflexes serve to protect the cornea from damage. With practice we can learn to inhibit these reactions – an important ability if we wish to wear contact lenses, or to open our eyes underwater unprotected by a mask or goggles. There are, of course, realistic concerns about the effect on our eyes of possible pollutants and detergent chemicals used to disinfect pools. People who are ultra-sensitive to chlorine or have allergic reactions to certain chemicals obviously need to take special care about chemically disinfected pools. Fortunately, there is a growing range of alternative methods of cleaning, filtering, and disinfecting pools. But whilst prolonged exposure of the eyes to chlorine and other chemicals can cause irritation, in most swimming-pools the levels are carefully monitored and controlled so that the water is safe, even if swallowed by mistake.

Anxiety that injury or pain to the eye might result from water alone being in contact with the cornea is misplaced. With its softness and neutral pH balance, clean water is a safe medium for the eyes. However, even when they keep their eyes tightly shut underwater, some swimmers feel the need to wipe water off their eyelids before they re-open them. The habit of using the hands to sweep the water constantly away from the eyes is often observed in beginners, but should be discouraged as it impedes learning to swim at any stage. Flicking the eyelashes and blinking the eyelids are all that is required for the eye to repel excess water. Familiarity with the feeling of water bathing the cornea – whether through regular swimming or practice in the bath (see the box overleaf) – helps to remove unnecessary and distracting concerns about getting water in the eyes.

Getting water in the ears is another distraction, but one which need not present excessive concern to swimmers. Reactions range from an irrational anxiety that simply placing the ears in the water will cause them to fill up, to an exaggerated worry about water remaining trapped inside the ears. The complex series of twists and turns inside the human ear effectively prevents water penetrating beyond its outer parts. The deeper, more delicate region towards the eardrum is virtually inaccessible. Occasionally water can be trapped by wax in the outer canals of the ear, causing temporary discomfort. If the water is allowed to remain there for an extended period, bacterial infection can develop, but inflammation is more often the consequence of excessive efforts to clear and dry the interior channels. Usually, water drains away of its own accord even if it has been trapped in the ear for a time.

Fig. 2.9   *Breathing out in the water – the first step in building confidence*

Countering the fear of putting your face in water

1. Accept your fear. Don't try to deny it in any way or you will compound your difficulties.

2. Be patient with yourself. Don't put unnecessary pressure on yourself by trying to conquer the fear in a day. Recognize that it is deeply ingrained and may take time to undo.

3. Learn how to exhale steadily and confidently into the water.

4. Pay attention to your orientation – how your whole body lies in the water – rather than your breathing. By redirecting your attention, you can gradually become more at ease with letting your face rest in the water.

5. Practise submerging your face in the basin or bath. Build your familiarity with the sensation of water in contact with all parts of your face, without rubbing it away from your eyes.

In the case of both eyes and ears, it's not just the physical contact with water that can be the cause of anxiety. Often it's because their functions – seeing and hearing – seem to be affected or impaired. This is mainly because the aquatic environment presents different kinds of visual and aural stimuli to those we normally experience outside the water. Under the water, sounds are muffled and sights appear less distinct. Some sounds will seem magnified: one's own breathing and heartbeat, for instance. It's important not to be put off from exhaling firmly and steadily simply because it sounds louder than expected. These sensations should not provoke alarm: unfamiliarity alone makes them intimidating. With time and experience, we easily become accustomed to the different quality of sensations in and around the water, and adjust our expectations accordingly.

Fears of placing the nose and mouth in the water are largely related to fears about breathing, which are discussed in detail in the next chapter. The question of how we breathe when swimming is of paramount importance to learning to feel at home in the water. The physiological mechanism known as the *oral seal* acts as an effective barrier to water getting into our lungs. We need to familiarize ourselves in practice with the operation of this mechanism, so that unnecessary fears do not overwhelm us and cause us to override it by our own undue efforts. Additionally, there are a number of swimming accessories (discussed in the section below) which can be invaluable in helping swimmers overcome their fears about putting their face in the water.

Once we have learned to put our face in water, we stand to derive additional benefit from the effects of another remarkable physiological mechanism, known as the *dive instinct*. The dive instinct was first identified in seals, who despite being mammals are able to swim for extended periods under water. It was found that this ability is linked to a measurable change in their metabolism, which to a greater or lesser degree affects all mammals when the face is immersed in water. This change comprises a noticeable slowdown in the activity of the respiratory, digestive, and cardiovascular systems. The cumulative effect is to allow for a slower release of energy and accompanying feelings of tranquillity – that is, so long as negative thoughts do not interfere and counteract these effects. There are thus positive physiological and psychological benefits to be gained from conquering the fear of putting the face in the water. Those who choose to swim with their heads held clear of the water – often, in fact, because of unacknowledged fears – are missing out on the very experience that could help to put a different perspective on their feelings.

Fig. 2.10   *Holding the nose will not help you to swim*

Chapter Two

LETTING GO OF FEAR

Apart from the specific fears mentioned above, people have more general anxieties about swimming. Some of the more common reasons – or excuses – people give for being put off swimming altogether are listed below. Can you identify with any of them? If you can, you may find that you also have reservations or unconscious mental blocks about dealing in a practical way with your difficulties. However, it helps to recognize exactly what needs to be addressed if it's going to present an obstacle to your feeling at home in the water. It can also help to be reassured that such thoughts are neither 'silly' nor unique to you. You will find that in practice they are shared by many swimmers and non-swimmers. They have to be taken seriously, if only because – especially because – they are your feelings.

Thoughts that put us off swimming

1. The water will be uncomfortably cold, or chlorinated.
2. The water will damage my hair, or ruin my hairstyle.
3. I will be embarrassed showing my body in public.
4. The surroundings of the pool appear unhygienic.
5. My swimming style will be a source of ridicule.
6. I am unfit, or my physique is unsuitable for swimming.
7. I will never be able to swim, or at least to swim well.

While some of these reflect an unwelcome reality which we may have to take practical measures to avoid or overcome, others such as nos. 6 and 7 are examples of mistaken beliefs – statements which may sound reasonable but in reality are not. Virtually anyone can learn to swim – young, old, fat, thin, weak or strong. The belief that one will never be able to swim engenders a reluctance and rigidity which is counterproductive and can make the thought self-fulfilling. Such beliefs combine to create negative attitudes which constitute a major hindrance to progress. It's important that negative thoughts are not translated into destructive reactions. There are various techniques for countering negative thoughts. These include learning to 'let go' of thoughts, repeating positive affirmations, and 'creatively visualising' a desirable alternative. Whilst all these may be helpful, the *AT* approach can be distinguished from them. It simply proposes that you learn to be aware of, and inhibit, the automatic psychophysical reactions which accompany such beliefs. The resulting self-awareness encourages you to explore and discover *any* form of solution which you personally find creative and beneficial.

You can usefully experiment with practical ways which appeal to you of overcoming negative thoughts and diminishing the discomfort involved with the very idea of swimming. We have made a number of suggestions in this chapter, based on ideas of becoming *familiar* with new and initially uncomfortable sensations, *exploring* practical solutions to overcoming anxiety, becoming *aware* of habitual reactions, and *redirecting* attention to use rather than dwelling on negative thoughts. These techniques conveniently enough form an acronym, *FEAR*.

Familiarity   **E**xploration   **A**wareness   **R**edirection

By bearing these ideas in mind, you can turn unproductive anxieties into practical steps to overcoming them. What were reasons for avoiding swimming become excuses. The challenges vary enormously between different individuals. Accept the challenge and create your own solutions.

Fig. 2.11   *Floating is fun!*

EXPLORING THE WATER

Learning has to be an adventure, otherwise it's stillborn. What you learn
at a given moment ought to depend on chance meetings, and it ought
to continue in that way, from encounter to encounter, a learning
in transformations, a learning in fun.

Elias Canetti

Just as play is an important part of how children learn, a sense of fun and exploration are an important part of adult learning. Swimming doesn't have to be serious
and solemn, or conform to rigid rules and procedures. Below we suggest some
ways of exploring the water, once you are familiar with putting your face in it.
They should be performed with appropriate supervision depending on your level
of ability, and in an environment which allows you the freedom to do them (not,
for example, a crowded racing pool). Think of them as starting-points for your
own exploration. Experiment, adapt, innovate, and find your own ways of being
free in the water.

Floating
Find out what the water can do for you, and what it actually feels like. On your
front, on your back, on your side, and alternating, discover how your own body
works in relation to the water. See what happens when you make yourself deliberately tense or relaxed, with your head and limbs in different positions, lying
motionless, or gliding after pushing off from the side.

Below the surface
Experience what it feels like to sink feet-first, or to plunge head-first underwater,
to rest on the bottom of the pool holding your breath and breathing out slowly.
Try propelling yourself underwater in different ways, e.g. using just the legs, performing a dolphin kick (legs straight, bending at the knees and kicking back
together). Note how much effort is required not to rise to the surface! Savour the
meditative solitude of being totally surrounded by water.

Twists and Twirls
As you manoeuvre in the water without a set direction or goal, you can learn a lot
about balance and how the weight of your head affects your movements. Become
familiar with the working of the oral seal: see how easily you are able to inhale
when your face is above the surface, and to avoid inhaling when it is under water.

TECHNICAL AIDS AND ACCESSORIES

Because a sense of ease in the water is so essential to the art of swimming, equipment that helps to promote this is a worthwhile investment. Adults who have difficulty putting their face in the water for any length of time can find good-quality swimming accessories invaluable. As the majority of swimming-pools use chlorine as a disinfectant (and even lakes and oceans may contain eye irritants), the eyes are likely to sting if they stay open underwater for long periods. To help prevent this, there's no substitute for a pair of good, well-fitting goggles. Without them, many swimmers will prefer to close their eyes the majority of the time. This not only increases the risk of bumping into things such as walls, lane ropes and other swimmers, but more importantly it contributes to a feeling of nervousness and of being in an alien environment. This is particularly true for swimmers who have poor eyesight to begin with. Straining one's eyes to see the end of a pool or to avoid obstacles is not conducive to feeling at home in the water.

Fig. 2.12   Accessories can help one to have fun in – and under – the water

For some swimmers, goggles feel uncomfortably tight or constricting and seem to leak and fog up constantly. In the box below are suggestions for ways of overcoming such concerns. Today there are hundreds of different makes of goggles on the market, and it's worth getting a pair that offers maximum effectiveness with minimum discomfort. If necessary, they can be ordered with lenses made to your prescription. Overleaf are some points worth noting about goggles.

1. When putting on goggles, place the eyepieces firmly in front of your eyes and pull the strap round the back of your head. It helps to create a slight vacuum in front of the eyes to ensure that they are watertight.

2. If the goggles leak, you may find that adjusting the width of the nose-strap or tightening the strap around your head prevents this. You should expect the goggles to feel very tight when you are outside the water. They will feel less tight when you are swimming, because they will be partially buoyed up by water.

3. Most goggles are pre-treated with an anti-fog coating. They should not be taken off and rinsed at frequent intervals, as this doesn't give the chemicals a chance to work to disperse the fogging.

4. Expect to take time in fitting goggles correctly and getting used to them. It's worth persevering as they can substantially improve the quality of your experience of swimming.

Apart from goggles, a number of accessories are widely available to help swimmers deal with their concerns. It's worth considering anything that serves to prevent distraction, difficulty, or genuine discomfort. A swimming cap is a boon for swimmers with long hair, and may be useful to prevent waterlogged hair flopping over the eyes and mouth. Although you may have to accept that they are uncomfortable and not always totally effective in keeping the hair dry, their main purpose is to keep hair out of your face so that you can attend to your swimming. Watertight ear-plugs are helpful for swimmers prone to ear infections or who suffer earache when the head is underwater. However, they can add to a sense of isolation in the water. Similarly, nose-clips are not recommended unless you have specific sinus problems, because they're likely to prevent you learning the appropriate ways of breathing when you swim. For hair and skin, shampoos and gels are widely available to neutralize chemicals and remove the smell of chlorine.

For children (and sometimes for adults), floats and armbands are commonly used accessories. But it is worth pausing before assuming that these are helpful for learning to swim. Above all, they can interfere with learners developing a sense of their natural buoyancy, the keystone of confidence in the water. While they may sometimes be considered essential for safety requirements, they should therefore be used only sparingly, if at all, in the context of children learning to swim under proper instruction.

CONCLUSION

Asked what the single most important factor is in learning to swim, most people would reply 'Confidence'. A sense of trust – what we have called being at home in the water – provides the foundation for us to do whatever else might come naturally in the water. As we have seen, floating, propelling ourselves, and avoiding the intake of water into our lungs are all things which do come naturally to us in the earliest period of our lives. It's a shame that so many people are prevented from building on these natural abilities, and learn instead to be fearful or anxious about water. However, with the right approach and support, confidence and ease in the water can be learned afresh.

We have suggested that elements of fear are present in most swimmers to a greater or lesser degree. Its effects range from an obvious and debilitating awkwardness to a reluctance to engage in a wholehearted exploration of the water's potential for pleasure. It's true that human beings are not like fishes or dolphins: water is not the medium in which we live. But it is more natural to us than we often allow. If water can never actually be our home, in developing the art of swimming we are discovering ways in which we can become more at home in the water than we might ever have imagined we could.

Dolphins, mother and child – at home in the water

the art of breathing

*Breathing is the hinge on which
the door of life swings.*
Zen saying

Breathing is vital to the art of swimming. A balanced and rhythmical breathing pattern is fundamental to discovering the joy of swimming and to reaping the full health benefits of being in the water. Problems with breathing, varying in nature and degree, are experienced by swimmers of all levels and abilities. However well you may have mastered the mechanics of a stroke, unless you have learned to co-ordinate the breathing you will miss out on most of the pleasures and benefits of swimming. The first step, then, is to become aware of some of the factors which affect your breathing, both in and out of the water.

What happens to your breathing when you swim? Do you hesitate to immerse your face for fear of breathing in water? Is there never enough time to snatch a breath between strokes? Do you dislike the sensation of water getting up your nose so much that you hold your breath as long as possible? Does swimming make you unexpectedly breathless?

While many swimmers readily confess to concerns about breathing, others who are not consciously aware of it nonetheless exhibit symptoms of anxiety in the way they swim. The anxiety itself is a stumbling-block to exploring ways of breathing effectively while swimming. Failure to appreciate this means that the need to address fears about breathing is often underestimated. This issue is surprisingly rarely addressed by teachers, swimming manuals and instruction methods. Straightforward, apparently uncomplicated, instructions such as 'Turn your head sideways to breathe' or 'Breathe between strokes' can be virtually useless, offering little enlightenment or comfort to the worried swimmer. It is wrongly assumed that we will know how to follow such instructions accurately and discover exactly how and when to take a breath.

Such scant regard for breathing is a weak foundation for learning to swim. Even after many years, poor habits and faulty co-ordination of breath acquired in the early stages can persist and mar the experience of being in the water. Learning to co-ordinate breathing with motion is not straightforward; on the contrary, it raises complex and important challenges for the art of swimming. It would be convenient if the only thing breathing required was for one's face to be out of the water. Unfortunately, this is not the case. First, even with our faces held above the water surface, there is no guarantee that we will not hold our breath, whether deliberately or unintentionally. In particular, we tend to constrict the free inflow of air, out of anxiety or for other reasons, by involuntarily tightening our diaphragm, the muscle which initiates breathing. If it were just a matter of nose and mouth being clear of the water, breathing would presumably be no problem in the backstroke – but it is! In fact, many people find swimming on their back just as problematic (if not more) for breathing as swimming on their front.

The rhythms available for breathing in and out are different for the various strokes. Each stroke raises specific problems requiring different solutions. Whatever the stroke, breathing efficiently in the water is actually a complex activity which requires thought and attention. Inhalation and exhalation need to be well co-ordinated with the rhythm of the stroke and the movement of body and limbs. It takes practice and familiarity to develop one's natural rhythm, which will vary depending on individuals' tastes and tendencies and should be flexible enough to adapt to different aquatic situations.

Breathing involves motion of the diaphragm, ribs and lungs. The diaphragm is a large dome-shaped muscle which separates the lungs from the stomach and other internal organs (*Fig. 3.1a*). When the diaphragm is pulled down and the dome is flattened, the lungs expand (*Fig. 3.1b*), drawing air in through the nose or mouth. As air enters the lungs, the surrounding ribcage simultaneously opens out to allow the upper part of the lungs to expand.

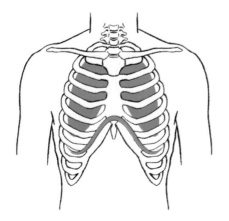 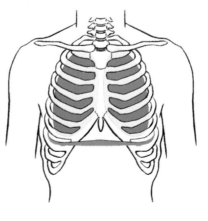

Fig. 3.1   (*a*)   (*b*)

A full breath is achieved by allowing the diaphragm to pull down to its maximum extent so that the lower part of the lungs is filled as well as the upper. The optimum action of the breathing mechanism can be impeded by such things as a hunched posture, an overfull stomach, or generally poor use.

When we swim on our front, as in the crawl and breaststroke, our orientation is potentially affected by the need to breathe. In order to take a breath we cannot avoid altering the axis of our head to some degree so that our nose and mouth are clear of the water. This creates an obvious risk of misuse. If we arch the spine or bend our neck backwards at an extreme angle, we not only risk straining them but may find breathing more difficult, because the body-position can constrict the lungs and obstruct the flow of air through the windpipe (*Fig. 3.2*).

Fig. 3.2

Note how pulling back the head puts pressure on the lungs

The art of swimming challenges us to discover the least amount of effort needed for us to rise out of the water sufficiently to make an effective inhalation. Good breathing enables the swimmer to integrate all the elements of the art of swimming: a relaxed awareness and confidence, a comfortable orientation, effective use of arms and legs, and a fluent stroke rhythm.

The need to pay attention to how we breathe is one instance of how being in water can bring about a beneficial awareness of our habits outside the water. If our normal breathing habits are unsatisfactory, as is often the case, this is bound to affect the way we breathe when swimming. Learning to swim can contribute to an increased awareness of breathing difficulties and how to overcome them. Discovering the advantage of breathing with a regular and flowing rhythm in the water has far-reaching consequences for the way we breathe generally. The regular practice of comfortable rhythmic breathing as part of a good swimming style is one way we can improve and strengthen our respiratory mechanism. Doctors often recommend asthma-sufferers to follow a swimming routine for remedial

Fig. 3.3   *In a relaxed front crawl, the swimmer has all the time he needs to breathe*

purposes, and Yoga teachers regard swimming as an excellent guide to developing a healthy breathing pattern. Furthermore, meditation and stress-reduction techniques employ steady breathing as a way of bringing about a calming effect on mind and body. Viewed in this light, the co-ordinated breathing which is part of a fluent swimming style becomes a relaxing and even meditative process for helping us recharge our physical and psychological energies, so that we can approach daily tasks with renewed zest and vitality.

BREATHING AND HEALTH

Breathing is the cornerstone of good health. When we inhale, we take in oxygen, which is not only essential to life but allows us to thrive and grow healthily. If this intake is obstructed we become prone to infection and illness. Exhalation too performs a vital function, expelling stale air from the lungs and toxins from the body. Weak exhalation retards this cleansing process: as well as leaving old air hanging around in our lungs it prevents the full and satisfying uptake of fresh air. As a result, the internal organs have to work harder to compensate for the lack of nourishing oxygen and to dissipate the toxic build-up. Common effects of shallow breathing habits include persistent skin conditions, an unhealthy complexion, poor digestion, and fatigue.

The pressures of modern life mean that most of us breathe in a less than efficient manner – too shallowly, unevenly, and with excessive effort. Breathing disorders such as asthma and emphysema are widespread among both adults and children. While these may be attributed to factors such as environmental pollution or diet, they are exacerbated by the effects of misuse. The improvement of overall use through the AT can alleviate and sometimes eradicate such problems. The effect of good use is to enable a healthier way of breathing through freeing up the operation of the diaphragm and ribs. The numerous benefits include increased energy and endurance, reduced stress, and improved circulation. The steadier flow of oxygen to the brain also helps to regulate mental functioning. 'Take a deep breath and count to ten' is sometimes proposed to help us calm down and allow ourselves to think clearly. In a state of relaxation, such as when we are asleep, our breathing naturally tends to be slower and deeper. Regular, unimpeded breathing of this sort has a marked positive effect on our emotional and intellectual well-being.

Equally, we know that our manner of breathing can be negatively affected by strong emotions. Under conditions of stress we breathe faster and more shallowly – in our upper chest rather than deep into our lower torso. Several automatic responses combine to affect our breathing mechanisms when we feel afraid or under threat. One of these is the startle response described in previous chapters. Another is the involuntary tightening of the abdominal muscles which often accompanies the startle pattern. The contraction of these muscles, designed as a kind of armouring to help protect internal organs from physical attack, forces the breath to stay fixed in the chest instead of flowing deep into the lungs. Our nervous system also reacts to fear by triggering an increased flow of adrenalin into the bloodstream. Such reactions are characteristic of the fight-or-flight syndrome, the evolutionary mechanism which enables mammals to face a potential threat or danger with a burst of unaccustomed strength or agility.

Fight-or-flight is of little value in most situations we encounter nowadays. This unconscious pattern of behaviour, like the startle response, is more likely to be an obstacle to efficient functioning under normal circumstances. Even where special strength and agility are required it may hamper an effective response: martial arts such as Tai Chi stress the importance of full, diaphragmatic breathing for access to vital energy. Our inherited automatic reflexes do not differentiate between situations of danger and moments of emotional stress. It's hardly appropriate to react to criticism or embarrassment as if we were facing the prospect of a physical assault. But all too often we allow ourselves to overreact physically to circumstances in which our mental equilibrium is affected. The constant repetition of fight-or-flight reactions is detrimental to both health and clarity of thought. The cumulative effect is to dull our sensitivity and make us tired and edgy. Learning to breathe efficiently under normal circumstances is a vital step in reversing the tendency to get caught up in this negative cycle.

Breathing is one area where the intervention of conscious awareness can have an immediate impact.

What are you doing as you read these words? Are you becoming more aware of your breathing pattern? When you think about the need to breathe deeply, do you sit up or try to change your posture? Do you recognise the relationship between the way you sit or stand and how you breathe?

Under different circumstances the pattern of our breathing alters automatically. When engaged in high levels of activity we require more oxygen, and our breathing rate increases accordingly. Our hearts pump faster to allow the oxygenated blood in our veins to feed our working muscles. We produce a greater volume of carbon dioxide, a waste gas that has to be expelled from our body by more rapid exhalation. Conversely, when we sleep, our heartrate falls and our breathing slows down. A similar metabolic change takes place when we swim with our faces in the water. This is the effect of the dive instinct, as described in Chapter 2, a factor which, if we allow it to, naturally affects our breathing rate when we swim. It works to slow down our breathing along with our heartbeat, helping to reduce stress and promote a sense of calmness and well-being. Of course, this can only be experienced if we are confident and relaxed with our faces submerged in the water – another good reason for mastering this requirement of the swimmer's art.

Fig. 3.4   *An open mouth underwater need not let water in*

THE ALEXANDER TECHNIQUE AND BREATHING

You would have found, certainly in Sydney in 1904, that if you'd gone to anybody who knew Alexander and you'd said, 'Well, what does this chap do? What's it all about?' they'd have looked at you in surprise and they'd have said 'Well, of course, he's the breathing fellow. He's the chap who can really show us what breathing is all about'.

Walter Carrington

The AT emphasises that good breathing is the natural consequence of good use. It's not a question of trying to control your breathing mechanism. When the torso is allowed to lengthen and widen, we create more space for our lungs to expand. We are all born with the ability to breathe in this free and unrestricted way. Unfortunately we learn habits of poor breathing as we grow up. Observe the gentle and relaxed way in which infants breathe. Their soft tummies expand effortlessly with each inhalation, and release back as they breathe out. Their heads remain poised and pivot freely on their shoulders. The ease they exhibit contrasts starkly with the way most adults breathe. We yawn or strain to obtain a fuller breath by lifting our chests or our shoulders, rather than letting our backs lengthen and widen. And we rarely allow our abdomens to relax.

One reason for this is the critical attitude exhibited in our society to the appearance of a relaxed stomach. Other societies are more sensible. The fashionable body-image promoted in contemporary Western culture militates against good use, and consequently against effective breathing. Images of fashion models with unnaturally flat stomachs are pervasive. Men too are encouraged to aspire to an excessively muscular physique, without regard to the distorted body-image which this

Fig. 3.5   Breathing is easy!

Fig. 3.6   *The crunch*

frequently results in – an overdeveloped torso held up by an uncomfortably narrow waist. Appeals to our vanity can make us feel that we need to hold in our stomachs constantly, though the actual effect this has on our shape is usually imperceptible to others. More importantly, it's a habit which is likely to harm our dynamic balance. It creates a tendency to fix our muscles which affects both our use and our breathing apparatus. The ways in which we are encouraged to pursue 'fitness' often compound this tendency. Truly effective breathing requires our diaphragm and ribs to be able to move freely and without rigidity, the numerous different sets of muscles and joints working smoothly in tandem. F. M. Alexander described the sense of ease that good use brings to the process of breathing with the image of 'floating ribs'.

Breathing exercises which require us to hold our breath, or otherwise interfere with our breathing mechanism, are considered unhelpful in the AT. Such exercises, when performed by people whose bodies are already unbalanced by excessive muscular tension and general misuse, are of dubious benefit. How can they encourage an understanding of healthy breathing under normal conditions, with all that this requires in terms of free joints and dynamic muscular balance? Take a person with obviously poor posture (*Fig. 3.7*) – rounded shoulders, curved back, the head back pulling back intermittently to take uneven breaths. When someone in this condition experiences strain in breathing, it cannot be alleviated, let alone eliminated, by 'breathing exercises'. The strain is more likely to worsen. Holding one's breath for a long time may force one to gasp for air, but it does not encourage regular deeper breathing and can exert dangerous pressure on the lungs and musculo-skeletal structure. Where poor breathing habits are symptoms of misuse, focussing on breathing in isolation from overall use cannot

Fig. 3.7 Poor use makes for shallow breathing

help much. People with breathing difficulties who are recommended to the *AT* find that their problems can be solved without using any breathing exercises whatsoever.

Most of us are not consciously aware of how we breathe, which is an obstacle to improving it. The recognition of a bad habit is a prerequisite for effectively changing it. But the recognition itself is not sufficient, because the force of habit desensitizes our bodies so that to us our misuse often feels right. Even when attention is drawn to our poor breathing habits, our senses are not sufficiently acute to work out with any accuracy what we're doing and how we can bring about beneficial changes. In such instances, the role of a third party, such as a qualified *AT* teacher, can be essential.

What happens when you are told to take a deep breath? Do you push up your chest and shoulders to try and breathe deeply? This action can create the impression that you are breathing fully. But the impression may be false. You may not be aware that the muscular tension in your torso is restricting the free flow of air and that you are only partially filling your lungs.

Genuine improvement in the way we breathe can only arise from a more sensitive appreciation of our overall use, and the application of the principles of good use in our everyday lives.

BREATHING IN THE WATER

There are indeed many cases where the exspiratory movement
calls for more attention than the inspiratory.
F. M. Alexander

How do you read the title of this section? The way you read it may say something about your experience of swimming. If you are confident and relaxed in
the water, it simply means 'how to breathe when you are in the water'. If you are
not, perhaps it conjures up an image of inhaling water into your lungs – in other
words, choking and drowning (*Fig. 3.8*)!

Being in the water requires us to become aware of our breathing and its rami-
fications for use. Because we cannot breathe under water, we have to pay attention to our breathing and how it is co-ordinated with the movement of our limbs
when we swim. But a number of factors distinguish the way we breathe when in
water from the way we breathe on dry land. First, in the water we obviously need
to make sure that we avoid inhaling water along with air. Secondly, in a non-
aquatic environment we normally breathe in mainly through the nose, which is
considered the healthiest way to inhale. The nasal passage, coated with fine
hairs, acts as a filter of airborne impurities while regulating the even flow of air
into our lungs. When we swim, however, it can be more appropriate, for reasons
discussed later, to take breaths mainly via the mouth. Thirdly, swimming requires
us to manoeuvre our bodies in such a way that our faces lift clear of the water to
allow us to breathe air in. And finally, the inflow of air is one of the things which
helps to keep us afloat, and which has implications for our body orientation and
for streamlining our movements. A steady, controlled inflow and outflow of air
can preserve the balance of the body, while uneven breathing can disrupt it.

Fig. 3.8 *'Breathing' in the water...*   *not 'breathing in' the water!*

Fig. 3.9   *With a natural snorkel, the elephant need not interfere*
                           with the relationship of head, neck and back to breathe

In swimming, breathing tends towards greater regularity of rhythm than under other circumstances, and can benefit from greater facility. Our breathing rhythm fluctuates constantly as we speak, move, or react to different emotions. But when we swim, various factors contribute to create the potential for a steadier and more rhythmical pattern. We have mentioned how the dive instinct works to slow down our metabolic rate. This itself can have a steadying effect on our breathing. Additionally, the fact that our body and ribcage are supported and cushioned by water means that we need to expend less energy to breathe. Another factor which distinguishes breathing when water-borne from breathing in other contexts is that when we breathe out, blowing into the water, our senses can seem to be more sharply focussed than usual. The sight, sound, and feel of exhalation into water can be initially unfamiliar and even alarming. As a result, some swimmers never allow themselves to breathe out with sufficient force, and can be taken aback by the noise and turbulence that is generated when they do so. But exhalation into water actually needs to take into account the fact that countervailing water pressure is considerably greater than atmospheric pressure. This doesn't meant that one needs to breathe out with undue force, simply that exhalation underwater may be expected to take longer than breathing out into the air.

Some swimmers, such as those who are influenced by Yogic breathing techniques, practise exhaling slowly over the space of two or more stroke cycles. This reduces the perceptible impact of forceful exhalation, and can stop the swimmer learning an important lesson: the need for a strong outbreath. It's important for beginners to become accustomed to the different sensations aroused by exhalation into the water. Have fun blowing bubbles. Breathe out confidently, and don't worry about the noise it makes. Fear of causing disturbance is a quite inappropriate reason for holding back from a full exhalation. How often are you disturbed by the sound of other swimmers breathing?

There are a number of other factors, often unconscious, which prevent confident exhalation. The sensation of water pressure against our mouths and noses can feel like a physical barrier preventing the easy outflow of air. This in turn can reinforce a mistaken belief that it's necessary to hold back the breath in the lungs in order to stay afloat. Others may think that the air in their lungs needs to be preserved as long as possible, in case they can't raise themselves up sufficiently, or surface in time, to draw a fresh breath. But this ignores the need for regular, fresh oxygen. Holding the breath in this way is a sure way of causing panic and hyperventilation.

Many swimmers are far more concerned to inhale enough air than exhale sufficiently. The emphasis should be reversed. Excessive inhalation can itself be a major cause of discomfort. If you take in more air than you breathe out, your lungs will be put under strain: they're struggling to take fresh air into cavities that are already occupied with stale air. You can feel as if you are about to burst. This is one of the main causes of the breathlessness experienced by many swimmers.

Do you complain of exhaustion after swimming a short distance? When you analyse your fatigue, is it that you're moving your limbs with too much effort? Is it because you're poorly orientated, so that you struggle against the water? Or is it simply that you feel out of breath? For most people, symptoms of exhaustion are the result of an ineffective breathing pattern. Learning to breathe efficiently can be the most important factor in increasing stamina in the water.

Steady breathing has a calming influence which helps in overcoming all kinds of anxiety – perhaps even the worry about water getting into the lungs. But it's useful to pinpoint the source of this worry in order to overcome it. Those who feel it may have experienced a sense of loss of control over their breathing the moment their face enters the water. This is often due to the belief that the water will rush into the lungs of its own accord. The discovery that this need not happen can be very liberating. We need to understand and be familiar with the fact that it only happens if we actively suck water into our lungs. This may seem surprising, but it is simply the case that we don't have to breathe water in unless we decide to do so. We possess an internal mechanism which, so long as we don't interfere with it, automatically comes into operation to prevent any water that enters our nose and mouth going further into our lungs. This mechanism is known to speech therapists as the oral seal. It operates by gently closing off the back of the throat through the action of the base of the tongue against the soft palate. This allows us, for instance, to breathe in solely through our nose – even if our mouth is wide open – by shutting off the oral passage at the entrance to the windpipe.

Because of the effectiveness of the oral seal in precluding the unwanted intake of water into our lungs, it's quite possible to inhale air through the mouth without taking in any water – even if our mouth is half submerged below the surface (*Fig. 3.10*). Indeed, this is precisely what allows swimmers to inhale confidently during the crawl without needing to distort the optimum streamlined orientation for planing across the water surface.

Discover the oral seal: In the pool or in the bath, you can discover how the oral seal works by inhaling and then lowering your face into the water. Let your mouth open gently without inhaling or exhaling. Notice that even if a small amount of water comes in, it will not travel to your windpipe. Experiment with how wide you can open your mouth, and explore the effectiveness of this mechanism. It even works when you move your head up or down, or from side to side, with your mouth submerged in the water.

Because of the way our oral mechanisms operate, it's far less common for water to get into the lungs via the mouth than via the nose. This is one reason why it can be useful for beginners to learn to inhale through the mouth and exhale through the nose. Sniffing water up one's nostrils can be a most uncomfortable and disturbing experience. When it happens, little can be done to counteract the water's passage to the lungs, except to exhale forcibly, cough and splutter.

Fig. 3.10   *Relaxed breathing – with the mouth partially below the waterline*

However, when we inhale through our mouth, there are at least three points along the oral passage at which we can expel any water that may have inadvertently entered through the mouth, before it gets as far as the windpipe: the lips, cheeks and larynx (the back of the throat).

Experiment with the way each of these three areas of the mouth can allow you to repel water. Rest a piece of paper against your lips and say 'Puff'. Even the small puff of air expelled is enough to move the paper, or unwanted drops of water. Secondly, fill your cheeks with air and blow it out. You can do the same if there's water in there. Thirdly, the larynx. Notice how the muscles at the back of your throat clench together effectively when you say 'Kick'. The same muscles can exert strong guttural pressure to expel water or prevent it from entering your windpipe. After all, what happens when you gargle with liquid at the back of your throat? You will find that it is quite possible to hold water in your larynx without it slipping down into your windpipe.

Case Study 5:   *Pete – Learning to breathe out*

Pete was a moderately strong swimmer who had no difficulty swimming twenty lengths of breast stroke with his head held above the water. However, he found that his back became sore. When his osteopath advised him to swim with his face in the water, he found that he became breathless after just a few strokes and had to stop. When he took swimming lessons, his instructor realised that although Pete inhaled deeply when his head broke the surface, no bubbles were to be seen when he proceeded into the glide phase with his face under water. Though urged by his instructor to 'blow bubbles', Pete found the noise disturbing and continued to hold his breath as he had been doing previously. He could not believe that it was 'right' to make so much noise under water, and he was convinced that he was the only swimmer in the pool doing so.

Demonstration by the instructor convinced Pete that the sound of exhalation went unnoticed by others in the pool. He practised exhalation in water until the sound and feel became completely familiar to him. Subsequently, he found he could enjoy the experience of swimming for long periods without the sense of strain that had resulted from holding his breath – and without the inevitable sore back.

BREATHING WITH EASE

The principles of breathing which we have been discussing show that the subject merits far greater consideration, particularly in relation to swimming, than is usually given. In the water, of course, the test of effective breathing is to be able to swim without worrying about it at all. It should feel as if an easy and regular breathing rhythm is integral to the stroke and does not demand any particular effort. Rather like driving a car or accomplishing any co-ordination skill, the initial attention to detail gives way to a greater familiarity with the process that puts all the various aspects of the activity into perspective. The AT encourages a flexible approach that allows us to discover what may be appropriate to any situation or activity. In particular, the fact that exhalation in the water requires more force than inhalation is something that needs to be explored in practice.

Ironically, the very effort of focussing intently on breathing can lead to counter productive tension. In this respect it's worth remembering the lessons of non-doing and redirection. By thinking of eliminating the ways in which we interfere with effective action, rather than by trying to act correctly, we can allow our attention to be redirected so that automatic habits are not constantly repeated. Attending to the experience of being in the water, rather than trying to control the actual process of breathing, is an example of such redirection. This can be particularly useful for beginners or for swimmers seeking to overcome the anxiety about their faces being immersed in the water. Redirection can be beneficial in any learning activity. A Russian proverb says 'We learn to skate in the summer and to swim in the winter'. The meaning is that the real learning takes place when we are not concentrating on it. This principle is similar to the AT principle of 'letting go of the wrong so that the right can emerge', and can be incorporated with benefit into all learning and self-instruction.

Do you worry about breathing out when your face is under water? Instead of worrying about breathing, focus on the orientation of your body. Explore the sensation of a streamlined glide with your face in the water. This is a most effective way of helping swimmers to overcome inhibitions about breathing out into the water. By redirecting your attention, you get used to your face being immersed almost without realising it. From there it's a short step to enjoying the sensation of plunging your face into the water. Then, you can explore different ways of breathing out strongly into the water and coming up rhythmically to inhale. Discover your own rhythms in the different strokes. Do you find it more comfortable to breathe out after every cycle (two arm-actions) of the crawl, or after two cycles?

Swimmers sometimes find that the problem is not so much at the point of putting the face in the water as when the time comes to bring it out. At that point, many swimmers behave as if their head were submerged metres below the surface. Not surprisingly, then, they experience a sense of haste and panic about bringing it out. Snatching the head out of the water often leads to a premature inhalation, usually combined with gulping in an excessive amount of air. Both these actions can cause water to be sucked in to the lungs, with all the attendant discomfort.

It's important not to rush the inhalation in any stroke, but first to let the water around the mouth and nose run away or be expelled by the lips and nostrils. This short hesitation is not the same as holding the breath, but is a considered, preparatory manoeuvre before breathing in. It provides a space – a split second is enough – in which the necessary mental and physical preparation for the action of inhaling can take place.

Even when the face is submerged, some swimmers exhibit their lack of confidence by breathing out in a jerky or intermittent manner, instead of making a strong, consistent outward exhalation. Because of an automatic tendency to compensate for out-breaths with equivalent in-breaths, such a practice can lead to the uncontrolled intake of water. To prevent the potential for mishap, exhalation into the water should be practised so that it is unhurried, even and sustained. This can circumvent a whole range of breathing difficulties. Some swimmers reason that because their nostrils are situated higher than their mouth, it is easier to breathe in through the nose and blow out through the mouth. Outside the water, we tend to breathe in through the nose and out through both nose and mouth. But when swimming, however we choose to breathe out, if we're worried about water getting to the windpipe it's advisable to practise breathing in through the mouth (*Fig 3.11*).

Fig 3.11   *Breathing close to the water*

Different factors interfere with easy breathing in the water. At an advanced level, for example, trying too hard to swim fast can produce a lot of tension which has a direct effect on breathing. For instance, the hunched, narrowed shoulders that characterise the competitive model of the breaststroker at the point of inhalation reduces the potential area available for intake of air, making it harder to take a full breath without effort (*Fig. 3.12*). A stiff, tense body also impedes comfortable breathing and restricts our ability both to float and to move through the water. The rigid use of limbs and general muscular tension actually encourages

Fig. 3.12   *Hunching the shoulders in competitive breast stroke*

us to hold our breath rather than let it flow freely. Some coaches and swimmers take breath-holding to extremes and justify practices that have little bearing on swimming as an art. Competitive swimming techniques include the practice of deliberately starving the body of oxygen – so-called hypoxic training – in the belief that it magnifies the effects of strenuous activity and is therefore a more intensive method. Whatever results this practice is alleged to achieve, it is undoubtedly prejudicial to both health and enjoyment. Holding the breath for extended periods of vigorous activity – whether with full or empty lungs – puts the body under considerable and unnecessary strain. It may marginally improve the racing speed of the sprint-swimmer, but risks damaging his or her lungs and ability to breathe with ease in or out of the water.

Just as each of the strokes has different breathing requirements, so individuals react differently to their specific challenges. Some swimmers who have an easy relaxed rhythm in the crawl may find difficulty adapting to an appropriate rhythm of breathing in breast stroke. Ask yourself which areas cause you the greatest unease. Why is it easier to breathe in some strokes than in others? Specific issues relating to breathing in individual strokes are discussed in the Stroke Guide at the end of this chapter.

CONCLUSION

For Rose [Murray Rose, the Australian swimming champion] swimming was an intensely
sensuous involvement, a rhythmic succession of sounds as the hands cut through
the water that passed under the body and formed a wave against the side
of the face. Rhythm reduces effort. Before a race he would listen
to particular music that was close to the rhythm of his
stroke. Glen Miller's 'In the Mood'
coincided exactly.

Charles Sprawson

While we live, we breathe. The regular rhythm of respiration continues without cease every minute of our lives. To recall the Zen saying quoted at the head of this chapter, life hinges on breathing. Awareness of our breathing is useful because it is always an aspect of the present moment, and awareness of ourselves in the present is the basis of the Alexander Technique. In this chapter we have gone into some detail about breathing processes that are vital to swimming. It makes sense for anyone seeking to learn the art of swimming to give detailed attention to the mechanism and rhythms of breathing, and to apply this understanding intelligently to developing effective patterns of breathing when waterborne. Conversely, paying attention to the requirements of respiration in the water can enlighten us to a new awareness of its function and effect in our daily lives.

We have emphasised that, for the AT, good breathing is essentially a function of good use. So long as we are well oriented, with both our mind and musculoskeletal system in a state of harmonious balance, we are in the optimum condition to breathe comfortably and fluently. It's clear that poor breathing habits in daily life can present an obstacle to developing good breathing patterns in the water. But it has also been shown that there are some significant differences about breathing when we swim, which we need to appreciate and incorporate into the way we swim at all levels. In the art of swimming, breathing is itself an art which requires understanding and practice.

Fear and anxiety interact in both obvious and subtle ways with the process of breathing, whether in or out of the water. When we're afraid, we tend to breathe differently, and when our breathing is disturbed, so is our mental equilibrium. The fundamental fear for the anxious swimmer – that of swallowing and inhaling water – can be greatly reduced by familiarity in practice with the mechanism of the oral seal. This is rarely described in the detail that we have gone into here, mainly because most experienced swimmers and swimming teachers take its operation for granted.

An easy and balanced pattern of breathing is the key to our awareness of the here and now. For those who enjoy swimming, the regular inflow and outflow of breath has both a calming and a revitalising power, complementing the beneficial effects of the dive instinct. The combination of the unique properties of water with the principles of graceful movement, woven together into a web of sensuous elegance shaped by the ever-present rhythm of the breath, can be a meditative and magical experience. It takes us beyond the pursuit of fitness and everyday concerns into a realm of harmonious sensation and artistic grace.

Helpful Hints

1. Never deliberately hold your breath when swimming.

2. If you find that you are holding your breath automatically, pay attention to the use and orientation of your body in the water. Is something impeding the natural inflow and outflow of air?

3. Relax your facial muscles, as screwing up your eyes and grimacing may be limiting your ability to control your breathing.

STROKE GUIDE I: CO-ORDINATED BREATHING

BREASTSTROKE

In the breaststroke, exhalation takes place as you release into the glide. Extending the arms forward exerts pressure on the diaphragm, naturally encouraging the expulsion of air from the lungs. Similarly, raising the body up and bringing the arms round encourages the opening up of the chest and lungs, thus promoting an unforced inhalation. Assuming that sufficient air has been expelled during the glide, air will flow in to the lungs without extra effort.

Standing up, bring your arms up to shoulder height and open them wide to either side. Think of the movement as starting from the back and shoulders and then travelling into the arms and hands. Notice how, as your arms open, there is a natural inclination to inhale. Now close your arms, bringing your hands together, and notice how it feels more comfortable to exhale as you do so.

Due to the pressure of water (hydrostatic pressure), breathing out into water requires slightly more force and takes longer than exhalation into air. A leisurely glide in the breast stroke should allow enough time to release sufficient air from the lungs for a comfortable inhalation to take place in turn. It's a common error to suppose that one needs to fill one's lungs to capacity with each inhalation or to breathe out every last drop of air. This is a recipe for anxiety and tension.

Fig 3.14   *Snapping the head back leads to inefficient breathing*

The length of time you choose to take in the glide will indicate the speed at which the breath needs to be exhaled. A faster rhythm of the stroke will require a shorter, more forceful exhalation. So when we accelerate our arm movements for the sake of speed, thereby encouraging repeated inhalation with every pull, problems arise because there's not enough time to exhale sufficiently in the short periods when the arms are in the forward position. The repeated pulling back of the arms without sufficient intermediate pause can create a tendency to hyperventilate, which is a common reason for breathlessness and discomfort in the breast stroke.

Discover your optimum rhythms by trying out glides for different lengths of time. You can set a rhythm for yourself in advance by counting, say, to a slow beat of four. Think 'glide' to the count of three, and 'up' on the fourth. Explore this first on land and then standing in shallow water: as you extend your hands forward, bow your head and shoulders and exhale into the water. Exhale counting three beats while your hands stay together ahead of you, and come up to breathe on the fourth count.

A common fault is to leave the head in the water too long before pulling it back hastily to snatch a breath (*Fig 3.14*). It is much more comfortable to allow the head to rise as an integrated part of the torso when your arms open and draw back (*Fig 3.15*). The pace of rhythm needs to be adapted depending on how fast you swim. Ultimately, the exact rhythm of breathing will depend on all sorts of factors: your weight, height, speed, orientation, or just the way you choose to swim at the time.

Fig. 3.15   *Lifting the head gently allows breathing with ease*

FRONT CRAWL

Many swimmers find breathing in the crawl harder than in breaststroke, first because the nose is closer to the water surface at the point of inhalation, and secondly because it is less clear how to co-ordinate breathing with movement. The mark of competent front crawl is the ability to co-ordinate breathing seamlessly with the movement of the arms and body. If you try to inhale too early – before your arm, head and hips have rotated – you are likely to take in a mouthful of water. If you raise your head out of the water too late, there will be insufficient time to inhale freely. Either way, you will interrupt the steady rhythm of the stroke. Unlike the breaststroke, crawl requires a continuous flowing action by the limbs, which is one reason why many swimmers overestimate the amount of air they need to take in. As in the breaststroke, there is no place for the deliberate holding of breath. Again, the exact rhythm or rhythms will be unique to you. Explore the options and experiment with rhythmical variations, allowing yourself to discover what works or feels best at the time.

Fig. 3.16   Without sufficient hip-rotation, strain will occur in the upper torso and neck

The front crawl is the only stroke in which the body rotates to the side for breath to be taken (*Figs. 3.16* and *3.17*). There's no rule about which side to breathe, but for the sake of symmetry and balanced muscular development it is worth learning to breathe on each side alternately (bilateral breathing). Right-handers find it more comfortable to extend the right arm and look back to the left, and vice versa for left-handers. This is why right-handed people are likely to prefer breathing to the left side (and vice versa). If you already have a favoured side for breathing, you may choose to refine your stroke before attempting bilateral breathing. But when learning the crawl, resist the temptation to breathe only on the side that feels more natural.

Swimmers who find it easier to breathe to one side usually incorporate a natural hip-roll to that side. When instructed to breathe on the unfamiliar side, they usually attempt to do so by turning the head alone. The result is that they tend to pull the head and shoulders further out of the water to allow more space to breathe. The hip-roll will be discussed further in the Stroke Guide at the end of Chapter 5.

Fig. 3.17   *When the correct rotation is achieved, head, torso and hips remain aligned*

BACKSTROKE

The most common complaint in relation to breathing in backstroke is that water spills over the face and gets up the nose, causing discomfort and disruption to the stroke. How does this happen when the face is resting on the surface out of the water? It usually occurs at the point when the arm goes back into the water. At this point the head tilts backwards, following the trajectory of the arm, and water rushes over the face and into the nostrils. The main reason is that the upper body is not sufficiently free and relaxed for the arms and shoulders to act independently of the head and neck muscles. Even so, there's no need to inhale water – it's quite possible to retain a vacuum in the nostrils or to blow out through them. Spluttering is invariably caused by alarm, which causes the swimmer to sniff in water involuntarily.

When backstrokers become fatigued and breathless, it's often because they are tightening their neck and abdominal muscles as an unconscious reaction to the anxiety that their faces might become submerged. It's as if they are using

Fig. 3.18   The habit of pulling the head back in the backstroke leads to strain, and can disrupt the stroke by letting water wash over the face

Figs. 3.20 & 3.21   *Partner support establishes good body alignment*

chapter four

leading with the head:
orientation & balance

Gravity is the root of lightness; stillness is the ruler of movement.
Lao Tzu

In nature, things tend upward. More precisely, living organisms have an observable tendency to grow and strive *forward*, *upward* and *outward*. Life is a continuous dynamic process, and this is one of the complex ways in which living things, including human beings, respond to nature's laws. The force of gravity is a feature of the world which both keeps our feet on the ground and gives us the wherewithal to grow upwards. Although gravity seems to bear down on us relentlessly, life on earth also flourishes *because* of gravity. It allows us to develop healthily, helping to shape and form our bodies like wood turned on a lathe. In a weightless environment plants grow misshapen and poorly. It's as if they have lost their natural sense of direction.

This upward sense of direction, or **orientation**, separates the living from the dead, the organic from the inert, the healthy from the sick. It exists on many levels: conscious and unconscious, physical and psychological, literal and metaphorical. The inclination towards positive growth is a defining element of human nature, balanced by a desire to maintain our equilibrium through change. But every moment of our lives we are subject to, and often actively resist, forces which threaten to unbalance us and pull us down. All change involves a degree of destabilisation. The *AT* offers practical guidance in handling these competing forces within and without. At the core of the Technique is the insight that how we orient ourselves – the basis of good *use* – is intimately connected with our mental and physical responses to the environment. The practice of the *AT* helps us to discover a better orientation and balance, with far-reaching consequences both for the way we move and for how we choose to lead our lives.

How are orientation and balance connected? They are really the same thing, looked at from a different perspective. Visualize a pair of scales. At rest it consists of two basic elements in dynamic opposition to each other – the fulcrum and the beam. They can only function properly when the base provides a steady central balancing-point. The beam rests in equilibrium on a fulcrum that exerts a countervailing upward force. A change in the position of the base requires a corresponding adjustment of the beam. This image can be applied to the way our bodies work as we move. The spine provides the upward thrust that allows our upper body to balance naturally, in continuous fluid realignment as we move. Orientation and balance are two sides of the same coin.

Fig. 4.1   *Ai Chi: balance and harmony*

Although primarily conceived as aspects of our physique, the ideas of orientation and balance have broader implications. If we live with constant physical imbalance, the chances are that we will grow mentally unbalanced as well. A sense of orientation grounds us as living organisms and allows for balanced growth and change. Thus the healthy response to our physical environment lays the basis for a healthy outlook on life.

The ideas of orientation and balance have great significance for the art of swimming. Water offers us a special medium in which to explore the way we use ourselves. Because swimming is performed in a horizontal plane, gravity acts on our body in a different way from when we walk upright. It is also counteracted by the water's buoyancy. This can act as an aid, if we allow it, to giving us a sense of a beneficial forward-and-outward orientation. Conversely, if we resist the natural properties of the water in relation to our bodies, the problems resulting from our poor use are magnified. We will find it hard to move or to swim with any degree of real pleasure or success. The habit of pulling the head back and down may pass completely unnoticed in our daily activities. However, the same tendency when swimming has immediate and substantial effects which are hard to ignore. The environment of water offers a greater opportunity to observe the effects of changes in our orientation.

The exact way in which we orientate ourselves to best effect differs between individuals. A 'right' position does not exist. It should also be reiterated that the forces and pressures acting on the body in the water differ in important respects

Fig. 4.2   *Pulling back the head...*

from those which operate outside it. In particular, the buoyancy of water means that the natural alignment of the head, neck and back is likely to be subtly different from good orientation when we walk or stand upright. Outside the water, releasing the neck encourages an upright axis of the head. But what happens if we release our neck when we rest face down on water? Buoyancy affects the angle of the head, so that when we release our neck, the head will be inclined *slightly further back* than when we walk upright on dry land. Underwater, the balance of surrounding forces acting on the body will encourage a different, straighter orientation yet again. But if we wanted to adopt, when swimming the crawl for instance, the same 'posture' as we present when standing erect, we will have to apply unnecessary effort to keep our head tucked in. Aesthetic criteria used in assessing good orientation must take this factor into account.

In all strokes, the common tendency of jamming the head back should be avoided (*Figs. 4.2* and *4.3*). You have to discover for yourself the balance that allows you to swim with freedom and efficiency. A practical understanding of orientation and balance in the water enables us to explore our own relationship to the water, and brings us closer to attaining ease and efficiency when swimming. The new awareness gained from our experience in water can also be extended to our experience outside the water. In this way we can gain a vital insight into the importance of orientation and balance in our daily lives.

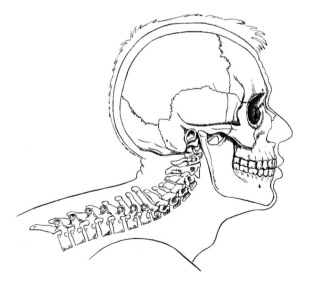

Fig. 4.3   *... squeezes the neck joints together*

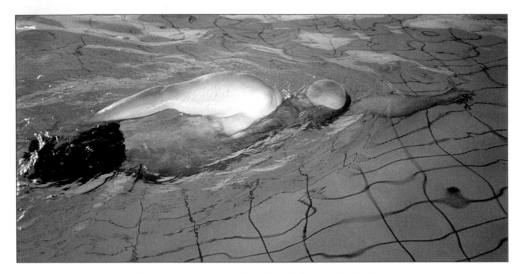

Fig. 4.4   *Maintaining a central head position as the body rotates*

Explore how changes in your orientation affect you in the water. Face down, push off from the side, keeping your neck free and letting your head lead your body with a forward orientation (*Fig. 4.4*). Now gently angle your head up out of the water. Observe how this encourages the back to arch, so that the hips and legs have a tendency to sink.

ORIENTATION AND THE AT

The dynamic relationship between the head, neck and back plays a crucial role in the way we orient ourselves. The main element of use that determines our ease of movement is the poise of our head in relation to the rest of the body. With the head as the leading element of a forward-and-upward orientation, there is a freeing of the spinal column and a consequent lengthening and widening of the torso which facilitates good breathing and generally balanced movement. In the AT the head-neck-back relationship is seen as the main element in good use, which is why F. M. Alexander termed it the **primary control**. The operation of the primary control can be clearly observed in the easy poise shown by infants.

As we grow older, the delicate balance which characterises the natural relationship between head, neck and back deteriorates. We acquire the habit of contracting our neck muscles as a defensive response to unpleasant stimuli. This stiffening of the neck causes the head to be forced back and down, which works against the natural extension of our spinal column. Our vertebrae become compressed like a line of railway carriages being shunted together when the brakes are applied. This is the first in a chain of reactions which combine to create tension throughout the body and interfere with our ease of movement. Ultimately the spine is connected by nerves and muscles to every part of the body. When the spine loses its upward orientation and contracts, the back loses its function as our basic support structure. This creates undue strain on other parts of the body, and we seek to compensate for it by holding ourselves up. Consequently, our whole musculo-skeletal structure is affected. The ribcage becomes compressed, constricting the breathing mechanism. The shoulders are narrowed, hampering the freedom of the arms. The pelvic region is put under pressure, affecting the ability of the legs to move with ease (*Fig. 4.5*).

The first step to reversing all these effects is to stop the unnecessary contraction of the muscles of the neck so that the head-neck-back relationship can begin to improve. By freeing up the point at which the head is connected to the rest of the body, the muscles of the torso are reorganized to interact in a more efficient and balanced manner. Tension is

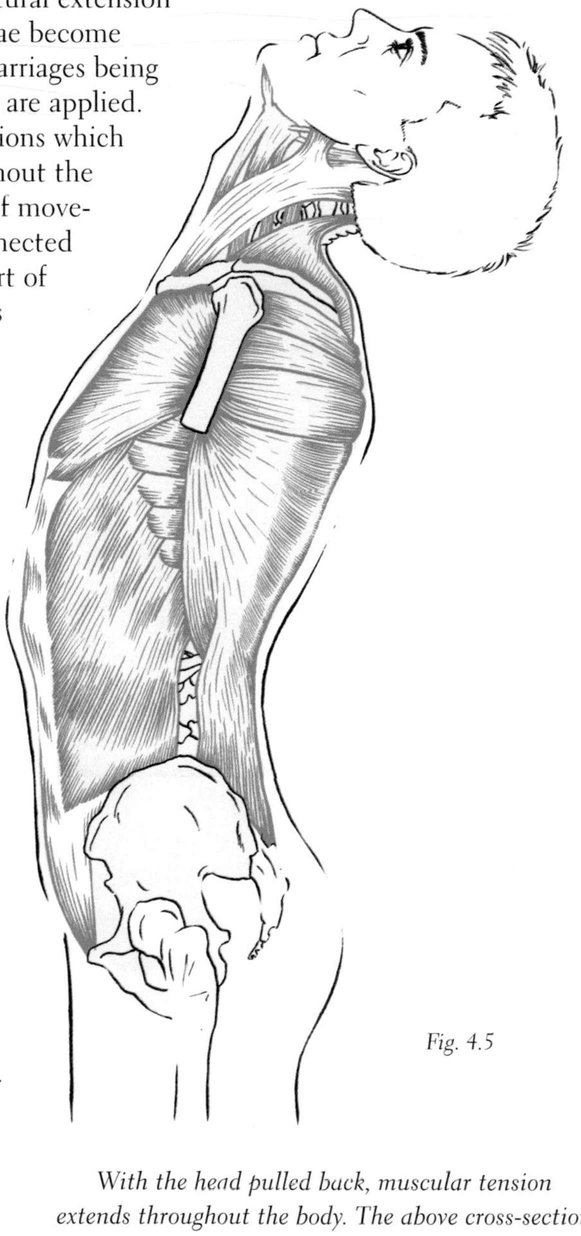

Fig. 4.5

With the head pulled back, muscular tension extends throughout the body. The above cross-section dramatically illustrates how a common position held by swimmers would be impossible for extended periods outside the water.

redistributed, reversing the contraction of the musculo-skeletal system that narrows and compresses the body. Because the system of muscles and bones involved is not normally under our direct conscious control, establishing the primary control is less about *doing* something to change than *allowing* internal musculo-skeletal structures to release. This is not a purely physical process: it also involves changing the way we think about ourselves. This connection is clear when we consider how emotions such as fear are regularly reflected in posture. A habitual attitude of worry or anxiety causes people to adopt a hunched, defensive stoop, while a positive, confident attitude has corresponding effects on use. We all know from experience how physical strain or discomfort affect our general outlook. Equally, emotions such as anxiety or anger produce muscular responses which increase tension throughout the body.

The AT respects the fact that mind and body form a psychophysical whole. Change in one is reflected by change in the other. True flexibility in our physical aspect helps us to be more flexible on every level. This is not to be mistaken for the limited kind of flexibility which arises from training muscles to ignore pain when the body is distorted into extreme positions, as in certain kinds of Yoga and stretch-and-tone routines. Learning to change one's use is itself a dynamic process. It's not merely a question of re-adjusting one's *posture* so as to hold oneself in a different position. The quest for a better posture can all too easily

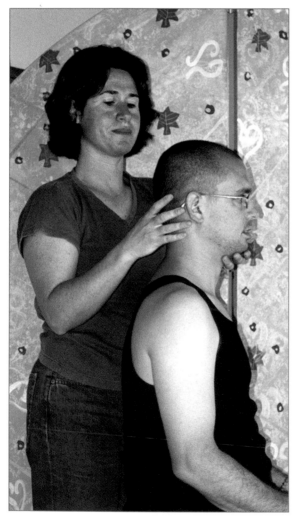

Fig. 4.6   Forward and up: encouraging release

lead to increased rigidity, and the adoption of a fixed stance cannot be achieved without muscular tension. For this reason F. M. Alexander cautioned against talking about 'posture', and words such as 'position' and 'stance' are also generally avoided in the AT. The classic 'upright posture' of the regimental sergeant-major – head and shoulders back, chest out, tummy in (*Fig. 1.8, p. 25*) – was justly dismissed by Alexander as 'an abomination'. It cannot be sustained without causing lasting injury to the spine. Constantly varying demands are made on our minds and bodies by the changing environments in which we find ourselves. In this context, no fixed posture can be appropriate. What is required is an *orientation* that allows for a truly flexible response.

Establishing the primary control is not a one-off action. Good orientation involves a living awareness of use that is renewed from moment to moment. Unless we're aware of our use, the inevitable tendency is to slip back into familiar patterns of thought and action. Most of us make far too much effort in our daily lives. Think of the range of our repeated daily activities: standing up and sitting down, walking, bending, dressing ourselves, brushing our teeth, lifting things up and putting them down. These actions can usually be performed with an appropriate minimum of muscular effort. But how often we find that they're done with an unnecessary level of accompanying strain and muscular tension. In focussing on a desired result, we all too often ignore the actual *process* which produces what we seek to achieve. The single-minded pursuit of goals elicits in us an automatic response to overexert ourselves. We rarely stop to ask how much effort is really needed, or how it might best be directed.

Because the intermediate steps to our goal – the process of action – is where effort is unnecessarily expended, one way of ensuring that we save our energy and only exert ourselves appropriately is to be constantly aware of our use during the action. The only way we can do this effectively is to be aware of our use even before we act. In this way, good orientation is the essential preparation for the efficient performance of any action. The specific method proposed by the AT to help us prepare ourselves so that we avoid slipping into unhelpful habits is to address instructions to ourselves which guide us towards better use. F. M. Alexander devised a series of messages or 'orders' to be given in a continuous sequence, both as a prelude to and in the course of performing an action. The sequence of orders runs: *'Let the neck be free, to let the head go forward and up, to let the back lengthen and widen.'* This is not an instruction for performing a finite series of tasks, but acts as a running prompt for achieving all the elements of good orientation simultaneously. It is phrased in a way ('let' rather than 'make') which emphasises that this is not about trying to perform specific actions. Rather, it's a way of stimulating us to stop interfering with the processes which allow us to be free. The projection of these messages 'one after the other and all together' (in Alexander's words) makes us conscious of our use, and offers us a means whereby we can direct attention to improving our orientation.

Thus 'good orientation' should convey the idea of a continually flexible forward-and-upward alignment of the head, neck and back, as a foundation for all further action. Patrick MacDonald, a graduate of Alexander's first teacher training course, illustrated the concept of orientation with the following image: 'Even though a piece of steel does not move in space towards the magnet, every particle of the steel will be oriented towards it. While keeping the orientation of the particles towards the magnet it is possible to move both the magnet and the steel in any direction, including the opposite direction to which the particles are orientated.' For instance, when we squat down to pick something up from the ground, we can continue to direct our body forward and up even while bending at the hips and knees brings us nearer to the ground. Even as we descend, we continue to extend. This is how we can apply what we have previously called 'thinking in activity.'

ORIENTATION IN THE WATER

Thinking in activity requires attention and practice, but its application has radical effects on the way we move and function. It is the key to breaking old habits and establishing a new way of acting. It also offers the means of developing the freedom and balance essential to the art of swimming. Balance here refers not simply to the physical aspect of our relationship to the water. It includes the idea of balanced integration of all the diverse elements of the activity. A balanced approach will prevent us, for instance, placing undue emphasis on any specific goal we have in mind to the detriment of our overall ability to engage in the art of swimming.

One way in which good orientation helps very directly is by bringing about a reduced resistance of the water against the body – in other words, making the body more *streamlined*. Traditional swimming instruction, especially in competitive coaching, lays great emphasis on the streamlining of the body. It is rightly considered to be one of the most important factors in stroke efficiency. Why this should be so is clear enough: you can make tremendous efforts with your arms and legs to combat the water's resistance, but if you're poorly streamlined you will find it hard to move through the water. The positioning of your body will act as a brake to forward propulsion.

However, swimmers can take the pursuit of a streamlined body to undesirable extremes. For example, competitive breaststrokers are often advised to round their shoulders so that their body offers the least possible surface area as it pushes forward through the water. While this may give an advantage of speed at com-

---

Case Study 4A: *John – Using the Head in Swimming*

John was a fitness enthusiast who regularly swam the breaststroke with his head out of the water. Despite exerting great force his progress through the water was frustratingly slow. The main reason was that the position of his head acted as a barrier to forward movement, so the power of his leg-kick was substantially reduced. The majority of swimmers who keep their heads aloft do so out of fear. John had no such anxiety. He simply did not appreciate that releasing his neck and using the weight of his head to help him extend forward would significantly improve his streamlining and his ability to move.

He discovered that simply letting go of his neck muscles enabled him to achieve tremendous forward momentum without applying any more effort than usual. Because he was not afraid to experiment and adapt his style, in a short time had halved the number of strokes that it took him to swim the length of the pool.

---

petitive level, it does so at the cost of healthy use both in and out of the water. The cumulative effect of regularly narrowing and stretching the torso is for the shoulders to droop and the chest to collapse. Such effects persist well beyond the swimming session itself. Once we start to discover a more sensitive awareness of the use of our selves, it's clear that the attainment of extreme speed cannot be the only or indeed the main goal of swimming. The desire for excessive speed is itself a symptom of the unbalanced approach to goals of no intrinsic value that characterizes so much of modern life. The pursuit of speed *per se* is a prime example of how end-gaining can have undesirable side-effects on use.

It is a misconception to suppose that without sufficient forward momentum the body is bound to sink. While speed can assist buoyancy, it should not do so at the cost of good orientation. Efficient swimming is a matter of using the optimum amount of energy to propel ourselves through the water. This requires two elements: reducing the water's resistance (or 'drag') against our body, and applying propulsive force in the most economic manner. Swimming with good orientation – rather than forcing our body into a more streamlined shape – is the key to achieving a constructive balance of these elements. The elimination of unnecessary muscular tension in the body encourages us to float more easily. When the body floats higher and flatter in the water, it offers less surface area for resistance. By promoting freedom in the joints and muscles, good orientation allows our limbs to engage with the water with greater control. It increases our sensitivity to where and when force should be applied most appropriately for purposes of propulsion. Orientation is not restricted to when one is upright. Forward-and-upward orientation along the spine can be achieved when the body is still or moving along any axis – vertical, horizontal, or diagonal. Furthermore, upward extension by itself is only one element of orientation. An equally important aspect is the process of broadening, which naturally accompanies the lengthening unless we prevent it in any way. For this reason, the attempt to stretch our bodies forcefully when swimming is misguided. Unduly narrowing the body interferes with the freedom and ease promoted by release and opening-out. When we swim, we can use the buoyancy of water to discover a whole range of different angles and positions in which our bodies can operate with ease. Water enables us to increase the spectrum of opportunities to experience good orientation within an environment that encourages us to move continuously. Holding our bodies stiffly limits our openness to such an experience. The art of swimming requires a constant, flexible adaptation of our bodies to conditions of buoyancy and liquidity.

USING YOUR HEAD

Freeing the neck and back allows the ribcage and diaphragm to work comfortably, permitting us to breathe in an unrestricted way. This promotes greater natural buoyancy and allows us to control the rhythm of our inhalation and exhalation (as discussed in the previous chapter). A properly balanced body reduces the amount of effort required to prevent our legs and hips from dragging us down.

> You can explore how buoyancy encourages a sense of good orientation by standing in calm water, submerged up to your chin. The pressure of the water supports the spine and allows you to stand without straining, your head free to pivot on the topmost vertebra.

The principle of good orientation shows once again that swimming requires us to be confident about putting our face in the water. Without this confidence, we're likely to interfere with our natural head-neck-back relationship. Ask yourself, is it really possible to maintain good orientation if we swim with our head held clear of the water? Perhaps it is, but only for short periods. Those who swim with their heads out of the water for long periods are subjecting their spines to damaging pressure and hampering the process of lengthening and widening. And people who regularly swim in this way usually complain of a stiff neck and aching back.

However, it's not enough just to put your face in the water. In itself this does not constitute good orientation. Even when the face is submerged below the water surface, the head can remain jammed back against the shoulder girdle (*Fig. 4.7*).

Fig. 4.7   *Pulling the head back causes tension throughout the body*

But good orientation cannot occur without thc neck muscles remaining free. This means that in the prone strokes (i.e. when we swim on our front) the head must be allowed to tilt forward under its own weight, leading to the lengthening and widening of the back and torso (*Fig. 4.8*). Of course, it may be necessary (e.g. in a crowded pool) to raise the head up and look ahead from time to time, but this can and should be done in such a way that the elements of good orientation are preserved. And as the set of steps shown overleaf for *Finding Your Feet* illustrates, raising your head up is *not* the first step required for the body to stop moving forward in the water.

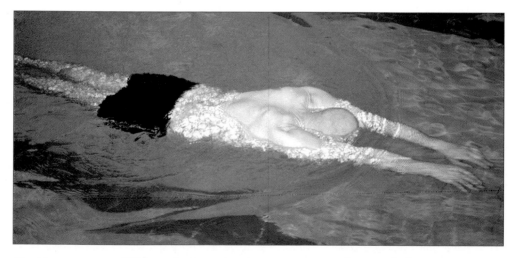

Fig. 4.8   *With good orientation the water supports the entire body*

FINDING YOUR FEET

Try the following set of manoeuvres for recovering your footing in the shallow end of a pool. This procedure is particularly important for beginners and those who lack confidence in recovering an upright position in shallow water after a glide.

*1. Push off from the side of the pool, hands out in front,
with your head in the water leading your body forward.*

*2. Bend your knees up together towards your stomach. Notice how this movement brakes
your forward propulsion and draws your feet downwards towards the floor of the pool.*

3. The common mistake of pushing the arms down and pulling the head back not only strains the back but pushes the feet back up again

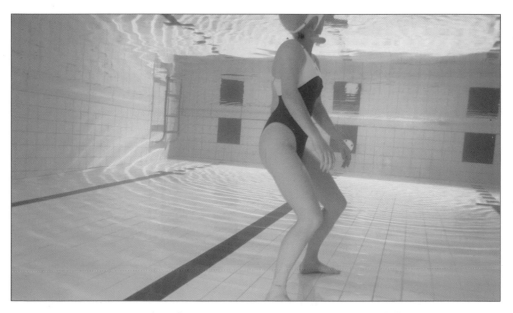

4. To complete the correct sequence, swing your arms back from the shoulder towards your hips and plant your feet on the ground.

Breathing presents a challenge to maintaining good orientation in the water. If we were able, like seals or dolphins, to submerge ourselves for extended periods without breathing, it might be easier to maintain a balanced head-neck-back relationship. But we need to inhale through our nose or mouth more regularly. Because this means our face must surface above the water, learning to incorporate it into our stroke without interfering with good orientation is an important aspect of the art of swimming. Attempts are often made to side-step this problem. Medical professionals, even while recommending swimming for health, sometimes advise against swimming breaststroke or front crawl for this reason. But the backstroke has its own complexities for maintaining good orientation. Some people think snorkels are the answer, but that merely limits the possibilities of the swimmer's art. In fact, it's far more rewarding to meet the challenge creatively, and thereby to expand rather than curtail your experience of swimming. There's great pleasure in discovering that it's possible to swim all the strokes and breathe well, without the use of props.

ASPECTS OF BALANCE

Good orientation in the water requires a continuous, flowing sense of balance. As we use our limbs to propel us through the water, the point of balance changes constantly. Holding the head in a fixed position interferes with this dynamic process. The point of balance at any one time depends on the relative positions of the various parts of the body, which are constantly changing as we move. One of the keys to discovering the art of swimming is a keen awareness of the delicate balance of our bodies in the water. Such an awareness provides the basis for ease and grace of movement, the distinguishing mark of the accomplished swimmer.

The body has a natural symmetry. Its weight is more or less equally distributed on either side of the spine. When we swim, the use of our limbs can either impede or assist the maintenance of our natural balance. If we pull harder with one arm without noticing it, we not only affect our ability to swim in a straight line, but disturb our overall poise. Similarly, uneven or uncoordinated use of the legs, which can be observed in swimmers who exhibit a 'screw-kick' in the breast stroke, reduces our control of how we move through the water.

In addition to these aspects of *lateral* balance, our body needs to find a dynamic equilibrium along its *length*. As with a see-saw, the weight of the head acts as an effective counterpoise to the downward pressure of the pelvic area. If we let go of our neck muscles when we lie face down on the water, our head naturally tends forward under its own weight. Rather than resist this tendency, we should learn to allow it to work in our favour when we swim.

Case Study 4B: *Linda – Shifting the Balance*

Linda, an accomplished swimmer, particularly enjoyed the front crawl for the sensation of speed and power. However, her experience was that she needed to kick with tremendous vigour. This alone seemed to prevent her legs sinking and dragging her body down. As a result, she was worn out after short periods of the crawl, and would relax by swimming other less energetic strokes.

In applying the AT, she learned to free her neck and back and lean forward into the water. As a result her balance shifted. Legs and hips floated more easily, reducing the need for her to kick hard to keep them up. She also became aware of another helpful effect. The widening of her torso helped her to breathe more fully, which improved her buoyancy and enabled her to release the muscles of her problematic lower back. These factors combined to transform her swimming style. In addition to speed and power, she gained a sense of rhythm and flow. She found that she could swim the crawl faster and for much longer periods without the usual feelings of strain and fatigue.

CONCLUSION

Most approaches to swimming emphasise the importance of body position and streamlining. As this chapter has shown, the concept of *orientation* is broader and its implications for the art of swimming are more far-reaching. In its widest aspect, orientation is about the way we think, act, and live, both in the water and outside it.

If we stop to think about our reasons for swimming, subjecting the body to the potentially damaging strains which result from poor orientation is unlikely to be one of them. Nowadays swimming tends to be dominated by competitive goals. Technical procedures treat parts of the body in isolation, instead of starting with an awareness of how our organism works as a whole. Instruction is based on measures for achieving speed, and performance in the water is judged by one's ability to get from A to B in the fastest possible time. Enjoyment, health and well-being are rarely the primary considerations. Principles of swimming developed for the competitive environment filter down to swimming-teaching at all levels. Efficiency is judged in purely external, quantitative terms, rather than our quality of experience.

But what is done in the pursuit of extreme speed is not always healthy or appropriate. Speed is just one aspect of swimming. Focussing on it exclusively shows a lack of balance. It's hard to find a single photograph of an Olympic sprint-swimmer in action which doesn't show the neck muscles unduly tensed and the head fixed back. Yet it's clear that such a position militates against the most effective use of the self. For the recreational swimmer, an unbalanced approach based on the end-gaining attitude of the Olympic competitor denies a whole range of possibilities that swimming has to offer. In particular, it obscures our potential for developing a healthier orientation – not only to swimming, but to life as a whole. The principles of the AT open our eyes to a radically different approach to swimming, one which integrates efficiency and elegance with balance and health. This approach fosters a new aesthetic for swimming style, and offers us the opportunity to re-appraise what constitutes the *art* of swimming.

STROKE GUIDE II: EXPLORING ORIENTATION

Different strokes require different skills. But while each stroke has its own particular features, all the strokes equally require attention to the principles of orientation. The ways we use our body in performing the various strokes raise distinctive challenges for the maintenance of good orientation. The purpose of technical practices is not to make you more rule-bound, but more free. An attitude of exploration keeps the process alive.

BREASTSTROKE

Breaststroke is often considered a simple stroke to learn, but the need for fine co-ordination of limbs, and the challenges posed for orientation, make it potentially more complicated than any other stroke. Efficient breaststroke can be viewed as a series of long glides punctuated by symmetrical movements of the arms and legs. In the action phase, swimmers pull back forcefully with both arms and pull the knees up towards the chest, followed by extending the arms forward while pushing out with the legs. Forward propulsion is generated by the hips and inner thighs, which push the water backwards when the legs are extended outwards and then brought together. This leads into the glide, during which the back should be allowed to lengthen and widen. The elements of movement and glide need to be properly timed for the stroke to be performed with fluidity and rhythm.

A common obstacle to swimming the breaststroke efficiently stems from a mis-understanding of the function of the arms. This is the only stroke in which the arms remain below the water-surface throughout, which limits the swimmer's ability to exert propulsive force with the arms. It should be appreciated that the main propulsive force in the stroke – around 70% – is generated by leg action.

Fig. 4.11   *Wide arms, strained neck*

Overemphasising the role of the arms sometimes causes swimmers to perform a wide, shallow arm-action, in which the forearms sweep back beyond the shoul-der-line (*Fig. 4.11*). This has two negative consequences. First, it means that the muscles of the neck and upper torso become the main means of lifting the head clear of the water. Secondly, the wide action of the arms tugs at the neck mus-cles so that the head is forced backwards. By using a deeper, bent-arm action, the body naturally rises with a minimum of effort and significantly less strain. Using our arms in an effective manner is therefore important for helping us maintain good use.

In the pool, practise the arm-action for the breaststroke by bending your elbows and pulling the arms under your body. Notice how this action on its own raises your upper body sufficiently to be able to inhale without your having to resort to pulling your head back unduly.

Fig. 4.12   *Lifting the head high out of the water is unnecessary*

When your arms remain closer to your body as you pull them back, your head is not drawn back as far. As a result, you not only put less strain on your shoulder girdle, but you can maintain your forward orientation more easily.

Many breaststrokers lift their head excessively when they come to breathe in, so that their eyes are directed towards the ceiling. But to inhale, your mouth simply has to be high enough to break the surface and be in contact with the air. Any higher is both a waste of effort and reduces stroke efficiency by interfering with the body's streamlining.

> When you get into the water, experiment with this aspect of the stroke. Find out for yourself how little you actually need to disturb the head-neck-back relationship in order to raise up your body sufficiently to breathe in. Compare your habitual way of raising your head with a movement in which your face barely breaks the surface. There's a fine line between raising the head just enough to breathe in adequately – and getting a mouthful of water.

The glide in the breaststroke offers the perfect opportunity to discover how stopping can allow us to release and naturally extend the body. Keeping the head pulled back interferes with this process of release and extension and impedes the flow and momentum of the stroke. Take advantage of and savour the opportunity of letting go in the glide. This is a liberating experience, enabling us to enjoy a powerful sense of release and natural extension as we move without effort through the water.

See how the balance of your body shifts when you change the position of your arms from by your side to ahead of you. Explore the different feelings by pushing off from the edge with your arms by your side. The shorter stance feels heavier and does not allow one to travel far. A longer body extension, with arms outstretched, gives a feeling of lightness and flow in the glide, and helps you slide easily through the water.

Competitive breaststrokers often exaggerate the extension phase of the stroke by incorporating a deliberate stretch into the glide. But what happens to your back if you do this? Overstretching creates an arching in the lower back and increases tension around the ribcage. Such stretching actually involves a narrowing of the back and compression of the vertebrae – a contraction rather than an extension of the body. This reduces our buoyancy, necessitating more effort to move forward. When we stop contracting, we lengthen and widen automatically, which is all that is required for an effective glide.

Helpful Hints

1. When thrusting your legs back, turn you feet outward so that the surface of your soles can push the maximum volume of water. Once your legs are fully extended, rotate at the ankle so that your toes point backward for a more streamlined glide.

2. Avoid using undue force to pull your knees up in preparation for the leg-thrust, as this action counteracts foward propulsion.

3. Never open your arms to pull back until the action of the legs is completed.

FRONT CRAWL

The front crawl (or freestyle) is potentially the most efficient and fastest of the swimming strokes. It is swum in a continuous, flowing action, with the head leading the body through the water like the prow of a ship. When you swim face-down (prone) you can allow your body to extend naturally and can use your arms with maximum flexibility for propulsion. This stroke offers a good opportunity to explore the experience of release and forward orientation in the water.

Efficient front crawl requires sensitivity to the changing point of balance along the entire length of the body. The alternate rotation of the arms allows the body and limbs to remain extended as they slice through the water. A useful image is that of a long boat moving forward without a break with a continuous rhythm of propulsion, rather than the push-and-release that gives the breast stroke its characteristic ebb and flow. Longer and proportionately thinner vessels are more streamlined than shorter, broader ones, and this principle applies equally to the way the body lies on the water. In the crawl, the arms, back, and legs are extended. The point of balance of this elongated figure is higher up the body towards the head, creating the potential for greater momentum (*Fig. 4.13*).

Fig. 4.13   *Maintaining maximum length for a streamlined action*

Snatching back the arms in a hasty manner reduces the potential benefit of streamlining offered by the elongated body. To overcome this tendency, it helps to continue to direct the extended arm forward until the recovering arm enters the water (*Fig. 4.14*). The arm should never become rigid. A slightly bent elbow

Fig. 4.14   *Both arms directed forward preserve balance and poise*

in the underwater part of the stroke allows for greater purchase on the water, and therefore a more efficient use of effort in propulsion. As the arm breaks the water surface for the so-called 'recovery' phase of the stroke, the elbow should be released so that it bends naturally. You should not make a special effort to bend or pitch the elbow, which involves unnecessary muscle strain and is a cause of tendonitis in competitive swimmers. Free rotation of the shoulder with a released elbow activates the powerful back muscle (the latissimus dorsi) rather than putting strain on the arm and shoulders. A free elbow also allows for a smoother and more controlled entry of the hand into the water, which in turn enables a steadier underwater pull.

Breathing presents the main challenge to retaining good orientation in this stroke. Craning the head and shoulders back to inhale has a particularly adverse effect. Unhurried rotation of the head and hips is all that is required to lift the mouth sufficiently above the water to breathe in. A controlled combination of hip and head roll is the essence of a fluent, elegant front crawl. You may imagine that all you need to do to be in a position to inhale is simply to turn your head 90 degrees to the side. But can you do this, even out of the water, without feeling the pull on your neck muscles? In practice, a hip-roll which initiates rotation of the torso gives vital assistance to the process. If the hips contribute half the body-roll, the neck muscles only need to rotate the head half as far. This creates more time and ease for breath to be taken without disturbing the balance of head, neck and back.

Explore the enjoyable possibilities offered by increased mobility of the hips in the following way (*Fig. 4.15*). After swimming on your front for a few strokes, roll your whole body over onto your back. Notice how much easier this is if you treat the body as a unit. Imagine starting the movement from the hips, instead of twisting your head and neck and letting your torso follow. Incorporate the sensation of rolling your whole body unhurriedly into the continuous action of the stroke. You can remind yourself to start the outward roll from the hip, and the return roll leading with the head, by repeating rhythmically as you perform the action 'Hips: – roll out. Head: – back in.'

Fig. 4.15   *The hip roll*

The use of the arms in the crawl, as in the backstroke, also affects orientation. Excessive effort with the arms can force the head backward. Since propulsion is generated by the arm-pull beneath the water, crashing the arms down into the water is both a waste of energy and militates against the control needed to prepare an effective pull. If the hand enters at a wide angle to the body it disturbs the balance. Equally, a narrow entry – when the hand enters the water at a point within the width of the shoulders – causes the body to wobble unevenly. When swimmers with this tendency first try to bring their hands into the water at a wider point of entry than they're used to, they frequently feel that their arms are entering the water significantly more widely than they actually are (*Fig. 4.16*).

The problem of placing the hand correctly on its re-entry into the water offers a prime instance of what the *AT* calls unreliable sensory appreciation. The faulty arm action may have become so ingrained that it feels right. When we come to modify it, to start with it feels wrong. Learning the art of swimming is a continuous process of development and refinement of motor skills. We should not, therefore, limit ourselves by relying solely on our feelings. A teacher, external observer, or the aid of photography can be indispensable to the successful accomplishment of the ideas and practices suggested in this chapter.

Fig. 4.16   *Keep the arm action relaxed and controlled*

Helpful Hints

1. Fully extend the arm into the water before drawing it back.

2. Don't windmill your arms, but bring one arm forward in a controlled action from the shoulder as if passing an object forward.

3. When bringing your face out of the water, maintain your leg kick.

4. Don't lift your head to breathe; rotate your body, starting with the hips.

BACKSTROKE

When performed correctly, backstroke can be the most elegant and relaxed-looking of all the strokes. However, if a good head-neck-back relationship is not maintained, it becomes disorganized and awkward. Some swimmers pull their head right back so that their eyes are focussed on a point behind them, which can cause the back to arch unduly and water to spill over the face. Others crane their heads forward too far in an attempt to hold their face out of the water. This compresses the chest and puts a strain on the neck muscles.

Backstroke is performed with a regular arm action combined with a steady leg-kick. The head and spine should remain centred, while the hips and shoulders constantly rotate, requiring a free-flowing mobility of the hip and shoulder joints. The legs do not simply kick up and down at right angles to the water surface. During the stroke they will mainly be angled to one side or the other, following the angle of the torso and lower body . The alternating arm-pull required for propulsion creates continuous alterations in the body's lateral balance. Controlling body-roll helps to preserve balance and freedom. Maintaining good orientation is the means whereby this can be achieved (*Fig. 4.17*).

Fig. 4.17   *An open back and neck contributes to a elegant stroke*

Practice the backstroke initially in three stages, to explore the optimum release of the neck-muscles during its performance.

1. Push off from the poolside on your back, hands resting by your side. Your body should be slightly angled to one side (*Fig. 4.18*). Release your neck muscles, letting your ears submerge, and discover how effectively the water can support your head if you allow it to. Experiment with minor changes in the angle of your neck to see how they can affect the way you float, noticing how holding up the head requires more effort than releasing the neck muscles.

Fig. 4.18   *Head resting on the water with the body balanced to the side*

2. Perform the same procedure with one hand gently supporting the back of your neck. With your hand feel the tone of the muscles in your neck as you experiment with different angles.

3. Perform the procedure this time with one arm extended behind you as you glide (*Fig. 4.19*). Notice how much easier it is to float with the weight of the arm helping to balance the body along its length. Does this position have any effect on the sensation of release in your neck muscles?

Fig. 4.19   *Extending the arm without lifting the head out of the water*

Unlike the breaststroke, backstroke requires taking the arms out of the water and placing them back in. This is a process requiring fine control, and unless performed with awareness and skill can have detrimental repercussions for orientation. The temptation is to arch the back. If we hold our arms stiffly or apply undue force, muscles become taut throughout the body. If the neck in particular is not relaxed, the head will tend to follow the movement of the arm round into the water, pulled both backward and from side to side by the powerful trapezius muscle which connects the neck, shoulders and back. If the backward movement is too extreme, we risk water splashing over our faces. If the sideways movement is exaggerated, we increase resistance to our passage through the water and may disrupt the rhythm of our stroke.

Explore how well you can control the entry of your hand into the water. While neck and arm muscles should remain as relaxed as possible, the hand should be carefully directed into the water, little finger leading. This requires a rotation of the shoulders and a looseness of the neck to allow the head to move smoothly on its axis.

Orientation in the backstroke demonstrates the importance of the sculling action which characterises most forms of propulsion in the water. Sculling means pushing sideways towards the body with hand and forearm so as to propel oneself forwards on one's front or backwards on the back. After the arm enters the water, the elbow should drop so that halfway through the underwater phase the forearm can commence to scull. To do this requires a relaxed flexion of the elbow: a rigid arm cannot scull effectively. Furthermore, if the arms flail like windmills or propeller-blades, their very rigidity will cause the strain and imbalance in the stroke that has been described.

Helpful Hints

1. Don't apply too much effort to the first phase of the underwater arm pull. Release the arm and allow the elbow to bend before pushing down.

2. Let your arm exit the water thumb first. The shoulder should rotate as the arm recovers over the water, so that the hand re-enters with the little finger first.

chapter five

fitness can damage your health

Four out of five people are more in need of rest than exercise.
Dr. Logan Clendening

High-speed travel and electronic media dominate our lives and continue to proliferate into the 21st century. They have led to a huge increase in sedentary occupations and have diminished active physical involvement with our environment. Nowadays we no longer need to use our bodies in the way our ancestors did. Alongside technology's undoubted potential for liberation, the achievements of the hi-tech age offer constant inducements to physical and mental laziness. In the wake of explosive technological growth, the lives of individuals are progressively alienated from activities which require a balanced use of the whole self. Our way of living and working encourages physical inactivity. As a result, the lack of adequate, regular exercise has become a major cause of disease and ill-health in the modern world.

Even when we exercise we want machines to work for us. Technology so permeates our lives that we have come to associate fitness with the latest electronic exercise equipment (*Fig. 5.1*). Fitness has become a fashionable commodity. Commercial organisations and the media continually reinforce the imperative: thou shalt be fit. We are made to feel ashamed for not being fit or not taking enough exercise. As a result, more people than ever work out, jog, cycle, swim, and indulge in other forms of exercise with fitness as their stated goal. The craze to become – or at least to appear – fit has led to a growing incidence of anorexic emaciation, spinal injuries, steroid abuse, and strained muscles.

On the other hand, many people still resist the pressure to get fit. They actively avoid exercise because it feels like a strenuous, uncomfortable, and tedious way of spending time, despite the insistent reminders that it can make a vital contribution to their health and quality of life. After all, there is clear evidence that regular aerobic exercise reduces the risks of coronaries, strokes and heart disease. It enhances cardiovascular efficiency and encourages fuller breathing, helping to regulate blood pressure and reduce stress. Better breathing and circulation boost mental functioning, and hormones such as the endorphins which are stimulated by vigorous activity, have a revitalizing effect on the whole

116

system. For most people, regular exercise brings about a significant increase in energy and vitality. As long as it is performed in an intelligent manner, exercise undoubtedly has the potential to promote health, longevity, and a sense of well-being.

But how intelligent are we about exercising? Surrounded by noise and haste, we tend to match extreme situations with extreme responses. When we feel we have gone wrong, we seek to redress the balance with something equally wrong. In the face of ill-health caused by inactive life-styles, our characteristically unbalanced response is to pursue a dubious ideal of fitness. So on the one hand there is unhealthy inactivity, on the other all the absurdities of the latest fitness craze. When we launch into activity, we too often adopt a second-hand, thinly considered approach which denies a whole spectrum of possibilities for balanced change. This pattern of response is what Alexander was thinking of when he made his paradoxical-sounding remark that 'the opposite of wrong is wrong.'

Fig. 5.1   *Exercise in a hi-tech age*

FITNESS AND HEALTH

Health is a state of complete physical, mental and social well-being,
and not merely the absence of disease or infirmity.
World Health Organization

'Fitness' is the explicit goal of most people who pursue a regime of regular exercise. But do we really know what we mean by it? Are we doing the kind of thing that is truly conducive to achieving our goals? A fuller understanding of fitness and a clearer idea of what to look for in exercise might make us adjust our view of what to do and how to do it. While exercise brings indisputable benefits, fitness is not synonymous with health. We know that we can appear very 'fit' but be quite unhealthy. When we do strenuous, repetitive exercise for the sake of fitness, are we aware of what is really happening to our bodies (*Fig. 5.2*)? The value of a fitness regime which is boring, painful, and may result in chronic injury is surely questionable. We are encouraged to think that a trim, muscular or athletic image should make us more attractive (or at least make us feel more attractive). But insight into what we do to ourselves when we exercise can provide the catalyst for radical change in our approach to the whole question of fitness and health.

Take a moment to ask yourself what 'fitness' means to you. Knowing what you assume 'fitness' should involve can help to throw light on how and why to pursue it. By learning to make the best use of your time and energy, you ultimately stand to enhance immeasurably the value of the exercise you take, as of any activity you choose to engage in.

So what is a healthy approach to fitness? A good reason for staying fit is to be able to take vigorous activity for a reasonable period of time without feeling unduly breathless, strained or exhausted. This has clear benefits for all sorts of activities we regularly engage in – climbing stairs, running for a bus, carrying heavy objects. Healthy circulation of the blood also helps us think clearly, and acts to ward off illness. Furthermore, cardiovascular fitness obtained through regular aerobic exercise increases the chances of longevity. But long life is only something to be desired if we remain in a condition to enjoy it. Staying fit through regular exercise can help enhance the quality of our lives by sharpening our faculties and allowing us to enjoy a wide range of physical and intellectual

Fig. 5.2   *The weight trainer's effort shows in every muscle*

activities into old age. All these are valid enough reasons for wanting to under-
take a balanced regime of physical activity.

A useful first step, then, is to form a clear idea of our aims in taking exercise.
Secondly, before embarking on a fitness routine we are customarily encouraged
to be aware of our overall physical condition. Such an awareness, as we discussed
in the opening chapter, exists on different levels. You may not be suffering from

any medical condition or physical deficiency which prevents you exercising. But are you sufficiently in touch with yourself, even when simply sitting or standing, to know that the way you choose to exercise will bring the desired benefits? Can you be sure that it doesn't pose risks to your health in ways that you have over-looked?

Take breathing, for instance. Efficient breathing is essential to good health and, as discussed in Chapter 3, a key element in the art of swimming. Ineffective breathing can significantly reduce, if not nullify, the positive effects of exercise. How aware are you of how you breathe? Do you know how your pattern of breathing changes during different types of activity? Or take the desire to look good. The single-minded pursuit of muscular strength and a 'good figure' can have particularly unwelcome side-effects. Are you sure that straining to extend your muscles is not placing dangerous pressure on your joints and tendons? Are you aware how excessive muscle build-up can reduce your flexibility, lead to rheumatic problems, and cause increasing discomfort as time goes on? Studies have shown that top athletes offer suffer from premature disease of the weight-bearing joints.

One reason why swimming is such a popular fitness pursuit is because it is thought to promote health and well-being without such injurious side-effects. It is recommended by doctors as a remedial activity for chronic conditions, and is considered a suitable form of exercise for all ages and physical types. The advantages of swimming over other forms of exercise are often cited as follows:

1. Water's properties of buoyancy and density allow vigorous exercise in water with a low risk of injury.

2. Swimming requires the use of the whole body in a balanced and integrated manner.

3. Swimming allows a steady rather than a rapid increase in cardiovascular activity, so is often recommended for people with heart problems.

4. Water has relaxing and therapeutic properties which help make swimming enjoyable as well as beneficial.

The pursuit of fitness aims to address three areas of physical capability: strength, stamina, and suppleness. When charts are provided showing how different types of exercise rate in these respects, swimming usually heads the list. It emerges as the exercise which supplies the best overall balance of conventional fitness requirements, as illustrated by the chart opposite.

	Strength	Stamina	Suppleness
Swimming:	****	*****	*****
Cycling:	****	****	***
Weight training:	*****	***	*
Yoga:	*	***	*****
Jogging:	**	****	**

What such a chart doesn't indicate is the level of risk presented by the different forms of exercise – their potential for strain, pain, and injury. In fact, any form of exercise, if taken to extremes, can have detrimental effects on health both in the short term and the long term. If we exercise without sufficient forethought or attention, there's always some degree of risk. The growing incidence of sports-related injuries has led to increasing recognition of the dangers of highly strenuous types of exercise, such as those involving weights.

Swimming is put in a category of low-impact exercises which are supposedly exempt from such risks. But there are ways in which even low-impact exercise may cause harm, if the effect is to compound pre-existing strains, tension and rigidity. This is rarely given sufficient consideration, and here the Alexander Technique has an important insight to offer. 'Fitness' becomes a dubious pursuit if our system is out of balance. Unless we pay attention to their use, virtually any kind of exercise can cause harm or discomfort, and will be of limited benefit. An example is suggested by the fairly common sight of people swimming the breaststroke with their head held permanently out of the water. Whatever bene-fit they may obtain from the exercise may be more than offset by the strain placed on the spine and the shallow breathing necessitated by the arching of the back (*Fig. 5.3 and 5.4*).

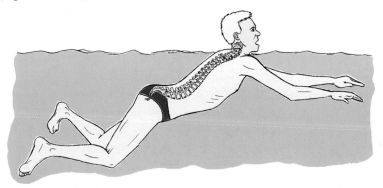

Pulling the head back causes compression throughout the spine and increases drag   *Fig. 5.3*

Fig. 5.4   *Physical elegance does not always lead to efficient form*

A similar objection applies to those who snatch their head back to breathe because their swimming rhythm is unco-ordinated. Swimming with bad technique can do more harm than good.

It's sometimes claimed that exercise needs to hurt to have any effect – the 'no pain, no gain' syndrome. Not only is this motto suspiciously masochistic, it creates a kind of psychophysical double-bind. To try simultaneously to inflict pain on oneself and to be indifferent to it is bound to be confusing. If we learn to enjoy the sensation of pain by deliberately straining to the point of excess, the body's natural mechanisms, which normally seek to make us aware of discomfort so that we can take measures to reduce it, are thrown into turmoil. So, by pursuing fitness in this way, we risk setting up a conflict of feelings which leads to an active blocking of our awareness.

Nor do we help ourselves when the exercise environment itself is not conducive to sensitivity. The heavy beat of music in group aerobic sessions, the hubbub of the gym bustling with noise and activity, and a host of other distractions can overload the senses and divert our attention from our immediate experience. Equally distracting is the internal clamour – the desire to look good, to show off, to keep up with others, to conceal one's figure, to avoid the tedium of exercise by letting the mind wander. The fact that exercise, and especially swimming, often takes place in a public environment makes such distracting thoughts hard to avoid, particularly when they are not recognized as potentially harmful and handled accordingly. One of the most unhelpful internal pressures is the urge to compete in the water, which is so common and widely accepted that it merits more detailed consideration.

LEARNING TO SWIM: THE COMPETITIVE MODEL

The world's top researchers estimate that champion swimmers owe about 70%
of their great performance to perfect stroke mechanics and only 30% to
their fitness… Fitness is something that happens to you when
you are practising good technique.

Terry Laughlin

The public image of swimming is shaped by what we see and read on our television screens and in the media. These are mainly competitive events in which the sole criterion of success in the water is speed. In competitive swimming, as in every other sport, records are being broken all the time. Sports science has revolutionized the way that top athletes train and swim, and human velocity in the water has increased in leaps and bounds. This is part and parcel of the modern world's obsession with speed. There are no Gold Medals for running gracefully or swimming freestyle in a supremely elegant way. The emphasis on speed dominates the way that we think about swimming. It affects our view of swimming at all levels, as swimmers seek to emulate the style and achievement of champions.

It's not hard to see that this attitude – speed at any cost – may be inappropriate for the average swimmer. Given that we haven't developed the physical capacities that allow top athletes to exploit their natural talents under extreme conditions, not only is focussing on speed more likely to result in strain, but it's bound to distort our understanding of how to swim more enjoyably and effectively at our own level. We unconsciously absorb skilfully captured images of Olympic breaststroke sprinters pulling themselves high out of the water with every stroke. Such overexertion may be one way of helping contestants swim the breast stroke faster in their single-minded race to the end of the pool. But the cost of doing so is tremendous pressure placed on the lower back and torso. How can this help you to attain a healthier and happier experience of swimming? It's far likelier to cause discomfort and possible injury.

Fitness enthusiasts often treat swimming as just another form of physical training. Reluctant exercis-

Fig. 5.5   *Lane rage*

ers also take the opportunity to delude themselves that swimming is an easy route to fitness. Given swimming's well-known benefits, the occasional dip, the routine 20 lengths, is enough to assuage their guilt about lack of serious exercise. Even those who ostensibly go swimming 'for fun' can slip into the habit of treating it solely as a means to fitness. Ironically, they may choose the water in the first place because they appreciate that swimming offers unique varieties of pleasure which land-based activities cannot. But nine times out of ten, their attitude to what they should do in the water circumscribes their ability to enjoy the very qualities that make swimming such a distinctive recreational activity.

In particular, we often observe people who think of themselves as good swimmers totally intent on covering a stretch of water in the fastest possible time. The water becomes an assault course, as they thrash up and down with unflinching determination and no sense of discovery or exploration. They may as well not be in water at all, given that they're using it merely as another piece of gym apparatus against which to push and heave. Exercising in the water for the sake of fitness all too often takes on the character of duty rather than pleasure.

The lack of attention to the moment-by-moment experience frequently has its origin in early experience. Such inattentive activity is often the unhappy result of learning to swim in a way which emphasises competitive goals. Many young children initially see the water as a 'favourite place' – a space to play, have fun, and experience sensations that are exciting and different. Fear of water is not innate, but usually arises out of negative attitudes or experiences in early youth (as discussed in Chapter 2). Many adults' reluctance to swim may similarly be traced to pressures experienced in youth. All too often, children who demonstrate a marked degree of ability in the water are urged by over-ambitious teachers or parents to 'get serious' about swimming. This can mean embarking on a strenuous training programme from a very early age. It's questionable how much a 12-year-old can benefit from being pushed to the limit of his or her physical ability for up to four hours a day. Inevitably, the sense of fun will be subordinated to a desire to swim faster or further than the next child. Although competition can be useful for developing skills to a high level, it can also be counterproductive. It implies that activity is not an end in itself but a means to some external reward. Official swimming-teaching organisations encourage this by promoting an incentive-based model of achievement – badges, medals and awards – which allows little room for initiative or creativity in the water. While such incentives work for some, for others they interfere with the discovery of personal enjoyment in swimming, turning it into a sport in which artificial, pre-defined ends hold more allure than the activity itself.

Loafing and malingering should be made to be undesirable qualities; such qualities should be socially ostracized by the rest of the team. Frequently we have used a 'hurt, pain and agony chart' to demonstrate this concept. I try to place a halo over the head of the swimmer who has the ability to work hard. The lazy swimmer who refuses to work hard drops from our team as a result of social pressure from other swimmers…The whole programme is designed to emphasise this toughness and manliness. All extreme emotional outbursts, crying, complaining or other overt and obnoxious acts are taken to be signs of weakness and are discouraged.

From the *Competitive Swimming Manual* by Doc Counsilman,
leading Olympic swimming coach and author of *The Science of Swimming*.

The competitive approach can become so ingrained that it's very hard to shake off in later life. Teenagers and adults often retain competitive attitudes even when they are no longer in a competitive setting. Although their skills may easily be adequate for them to explore the water's qualities creatively and in non-competitive ways, they are stuck with a mind-set of which they are only vaguely aware. Former competition swimmers are often completely turned off any desire to swim once their competitive stint comes to an end. If they do venture into the water, it's without any sense of fun. In their mind's ear they hear the urgings and criticisms of a coach or parent. They enter a pool with the fixed intention of completing their lengths in a given time, and adopt a competitive and even aggressive stance towards others whom they encounter alongside them.

The competitive attitude also produces a definite resistance to the idea of change. Any substantial change of approach requires a period of adjustment in which a sense of disorientation is likely to arise. Because competitive swimmers have developed vested interests in speed, change is particularly hard for them. They are afraid they will be taking a backward step if they drop their focus on speed. But when they allow themselves to do so, they awaken to a whole new realm of enjoyment. For practised competitors, an art of swimming which removes the emphasis on goals can arouse a new and unfamiliar pleasure in the creative exploration of their hard-won aquatic skills.

Case Study 5A: *Jason – Learning to Win Again*

Jason was referred to the Alexander Technique with back problems connected to years of competitive swimming. A lover of water from youth, he had been trained to plough up and down the pool for hours at a time to increase his speed and endurance. The competitive environment gave him little room to think about the way he was swimming. In his effort to reach the end of the pool first he would constantly look ahead by pulling his head back, which had the effect of stiffening his neck and shortening his stature even while he sought to redouble his efforts to reach the far side sooner. The tremendous muscular effort needed to move through the water in this way put further pressure on his lungs and spine, resulting in chest pains and a chronic condition resembling whiplash.

As a result he gave up competitive swimming. But whenever he entered the water he found it hard to resist his competitive training, and would swim at full stretch regardless of the consequences. At a reunion of his swimming team he noted a general consensus that the strain of competitive swimming had put most of them off swimming altogether.

Learning the Alexander Technique encouraged Jason to rethink his approach to swimming. He realised that his back problems stemmed from his attitude, that of an extreme end-gainer. He gradually re-trained himself to swim without trying to come first all the time. The consequence of his change in attitude was an immeasurable gain. For the first time since his childhood he recovered the feeling of what it was like to love swimming.

AN END TO END-GAINING

Modern man thinks he loses something – time – when he does not do things quickly;
yet he does not know what to do with the time he gains – except kill it.
Erich Fromm

The fitness enthusiast and the competition swimmer as described above demon-strate instances of the attitude which in the *AT* is termed 'end-gaining'. Focussing on the attainment of a distant goal prevents us from paying sufficient attention to the processes involved. This both impedes our ability to attain the desired end and does nothing to enhance the quality of our experience. Exercises that are performed in sets, such as weight-lifting, sit-ups and press-ups, are particular-ly conducive to an end-gaining mindset. If we are concerned about getting to the end of the set of exercises without collapsing, we are less likely to pay due attention to the way we are using or misusing our body.

We have seen how the pursuit of fitness itself offers a prime example of the drawbacks of end-gaining. Although modern culture advocates strenuous exercise to improve our mental and physical condition, there is little critical debate about the benefits it is alleged to provide. In fact, even a little more sensitivity to the working of our organism as a whole enables us to notice how fitness regimes can work against our natural balance. Exercise programmes tend to reinforce bad habits and misuse, and the tendency to stiffen the neck and pull the head back is exag-gerated as the speed of movement or the effort required increases (*Fig. 5.7*).

Fig. 5.7   *Cyclists need to be well-oriented to avoid a stiff neck*

127

Some routines deliberately treat us like machines whose component parts can be worked on and built up in isolation from the functioning of the whole. Mechanical activity which isolates individual muscle groups in this way is bound to ignore the integrated nature of a healthily functioning musculo-skeletal system. It can result in our developing some areas of our body disproportionately, thereby reducing our overall flexibility and impeding the smooth functioning of the joints. Furthermore, such routines smother our sensitivity. The body's signals of misuse, such as persistent aches and pains, are ignored in the drive to improve our 'form'. It's not surprising that the incidence of exercise-related injury grows year by year, and that sports-related therapies – virtually unknown a decade ago to all except professional athletes – have become a regular feature of the modern fitness scene.

Sports medicine has identified a wide range of specific injuries sustained by competitive swimmers, such as a form of tendonitis referred to as 'swimmer's shoulder', and disabling pain caused by the erosion of cartilage around the knee ('breaststroker's knee'). Much more common is the unpleasant experience of cramp in the water. This is most often due to the inadvertent over-extension of less-used muscles in the legs and torso. Although swimming is alleged to be innocuous, it clearly presents risks of this kind if pursued in an unconsidered way. It's important to be aware of the potential hazards, and to know how strain and injury can occur despite the fact that the water acts as a cushion against 'high-impact' injury.

The support offered to the body by water, with its dual property of both yielding to and resisting our actions, certainly offer us the opportunity to increase strength and stamina while moving more freely and fluidly than is possible on land. Swimmers intent on achieving a goal of fitness rarely appreciate these advantages to the full. Their ease and enjoyment are reduced by the sheer effort of trying to swim a given distance in a set time, in an inflexible way. If their system is already out of balance, even the advantages of buoyancy in reducing the requirement for effort are not realised: the unhealthy imbalance is merely reinforced. Excessive effort and poor technique can actually do more harm than good. Swimming awkwardly can reactivate old injuries, aggravate disorders, and result in neck, shoulder and back pain.

End-gaining thus serves little purpose apart from providing a distraction from performing the activity in hand. Those who swim with the overriding intention in their minds to get fit, strengthen their muscles, or lose weight – typical examples of end-gaining approaches – usually have fixed ideas of what they should do to achieve their aims. Little thought is given to the way they move through the water; attention is switched off and automatic habits take over. This tendency can be a major obstacle to learning to be free and feeling at home in the water.

Even though the buoyancy of water in principle reduces the need for effort and can accordingly have a positive effect on our use, in practice few swimmers have sufficient awareness of their use to develop a style for themselves that exploits this advantage to the full. So if you have specific goals, be aware of how focussing on the end can actually hinder you from attending to the most effective way of achieving the desired result. You can take the first step to a new and healthier way of swimming simply by reconsidering your motivation for being in the water in the first place.

Case Study 5B: *Helen – Getting Fit to Swim*

Helen booked herself into a beginner's swimming course with the stated aim of getting fit and losing weight. She had a preconceived idea that the way to achieve this was to employ maximum effort, both as a way of staying afloat and of burning calories. She resisted all suggestions to let go and apply less effort, with the result that after several sessions she was still thrashing about energetically, but unable to stay afloat or swim for any distance. After several more sessions it became apparent that one reason for her excessive effort was a long-held anxiety about appearing to be lazy. This thought had led to constant, unproductive over-activity in her life generally.

When she applied the idea of not doing, she grasped that she would only learn to swim if first she learned to float. This involved letting go of her notions about getting fit or actively doing anything to remain afloat. Setting aside her determination to derive immediate benefit from water exercise, she found that she could allow herself to experience the sensation of being supported by the water. She soon learned to float with ease, and was able to develop a relaxed swimming style which allowed her to swim with pleasure more often and for longer periods at a time. Without trying, she started to lose weight, and her poise and body tone noticeably improved.

The method proposed by the AT of overcoming the drawbacks of end-gaining in practice is to learn to pay attention to the intermediate steps. This was called by F. M. Alexander 'attending to the means-whereby'. By eliminating the unnecessary pressure caused by trying to attain a particular end, one can become more aware of the moment and thereby achieve greater command over one's thoughts and actions – in other words, greater control of the whole self. The removal of an automatic end-gaining response makes it possible for a more mindful attitude to emerge, resulting in more effective learning.

A mechanical routine which smothers awareness by setting artificial goals is apt to suppress unarticulated anxieties in the process. This is another way in which the blind pursuit of fitness goals can be dangerously counterproductive. Anxieties remain obscure to their owner, only to emerge in awkward symptoms such as stroke defects and strained breathing. In the urge to achieve a stronger or faster stroke, swimmers develop awkward movements without realising it. In addition, problems of style which swimmers already display may be exacerbated as they plough ahead unthinkingly. Often only when fears are revealed clearly and explicitly can they be systematically addressed and overcome.

For example, the involuntary twisting round of one leg in the breast stroke (known as the 'screw-kick') sets up a negative chain of movements throughout the body. This places uneven pressure on the hips, lower back, and ultimately the entire spinal column. The tendency is very hard to eradicate, and can only be effectively countered by careful attention and the mindful practice of moving both legs symmetrically when lying on front and back, both in and out of water. Swimmers who remain excessively focussed on fitness goals are unlikely to be able to correct this often deeply ingrained and potentially harmful stroke defect.

Fig. 5.8 (a) (b)

A screw-kick affects the whole body, not just the legs, as shown above in (a). By not turning both feet out evenly, serious injuries can occur, especially to the knees, hips and lower back. A symmetrical kick not only maintains good alignment, it also enables a powerful thrust through the legs to be achieved without damage.

THE ALEXANDER TECHNIQUE & FITNESS

Unknown to ourselves, by unconscious mimicry, we set our pace by
the machine; and the pace destroys us by destroying our most
sensitive and delicate co-ordinations and controls.
F. M. Alexander

The Alexander Technique is sometimes perceived (even by some of those who teach it) as a system which precludes or even prohibits vigorous physical activity. But what mattered to Alexander is not so much what we do as how we do it. Nowadays we tend to lead our lives as if our head was not a part of our body. We imagine that our physical and cerebral functioning are quite distinct. As a result of the heavy emphasis on the mental aspects, we try to compensate by intermit-

tently increasing the level of our physical activity, usually in the form of set periods of rapid exercise designed to work on the body alone. In this way, we believe, we can bring the two parts of our system, mental and physical, into some sort of balance. The sight of someone cycling hard on a gym cycle, head bowed, reading a newspaper, exemplifies this attitude. It is assumed that the activity by itself can benefit the body even if the mind is not engaged.

But the separation of thinking from activity is fraught with danger. Mindless, repetitive action can be boring, pointless and potentially injurious. Such behaviour contrasts with what may be termed mindful activity, in which one's awareness unfolds

Fig. 5.9 Not paying attention to the means-whereby

from moment-to-moment – awareness both of oneself and the action in hand. In this mode, not only is one less liable to harm oneself through straining inadvertently, but the attention to the moment gives our actions a different quality of energy, productive of a range of positive effects both of a psychological and physical nature.

The concept of fitness itself, as we have suggested, is open to different interpretations, but it is usually promoted as the improvement of physical capability in isolation from emotional and psychological well-being. The latter are considered irrelevant or secondary, and as a result the pursuit of fitness becomes largely divorced from the way we think, move, and in general use ourselves in daily life. From an *AT* perspective, a more complete definition of fitness involves at least an appreciation of the overriding role of use, with its intimate relationship to good health and psychological well-being. F. M. Alexander was emphatic that bouts of strenuous exercise, practised in a mechanical fashion by people engaged in mainly sedentary occupations, could be harmful both psychologically and physically. 'The body becomes the scene of a civil war', he wrote, 'in a state of perpetual re-adjustment to opposing conditions.' In his view, exercise could not be treated in isolation from the way we use ourselves in our everyday lives, whether sitting, standing, walking, or lying down. From the broader perspective of the *AT*, unfitness and ill-health are primarily a consequence of misuse. Because every action we make contributes to or detracts from our level of health, the pursuit of fitness needs to be integrated into, rather than set apart from, the way we use ourselves in our day-to-day activities.

According to the *AT*, therefore, most exercise regimes are bound simply to reinforce bad habits. Someone who stands or walks badly is not likely to run or cycle any better: exercise will exaggerate the misuse. The potential benefits of a strong heart to an individual's health are reduced if other parts of the body are not working efficiently. Although aerobic fitness is important, it is only one aspect of the road to health and cannot be effectively developed independently of attention to such elements of use as release, orientation, and breathing. The awareness of these aspects, developed by practice of the *AT*, allows us to make a conscious choice about how we use our mind and our body during exercise – whether we 'think in activity' or succumb to automatic habits. In this respect, fitness of mind and body are indissolubly connected. Being fit is not a matter of external physical fitness alone, but must include the ability to think and feel intelligently before, during, and after exercise. From an *AT* perspective, any form of exercise should enhance, rather than detract from, the sensitivity and awareness of our use.

The *AT* approach thus creates something of a paradox, in that it implies that you need to be fit before you can get fit. That is, exercise cannot promote fitness

Fig 5.10   *Mindful use of the body: elegance and grace*

if we are not already fit to exercise. The way Alexander proposed to overcome this Catch-22 was his emphasis on attending to the series of intermediate steps involved in any action, the means-whereby. This provides a method for both thought and activity to interact with one another in harmony, without letting our thoughts outrun (or bypass) what happens in our body, or our physical actions blur our thinking.

The parallel condition, literal and symbolic, of our minds and bodies is suggested by the position of our internal organs. When our bodies are cramped or restricted, the organs are forced up against each other, limiting their ability to function effectively. The heart, lungs, kidneys, intestines and so on can only work freely and healthily if they are allowed to occupy their fair share of space. The congestion which results from misuse during strenuous activity interferes with their optimum operation. Equally, we need mental space if our thought process is to function at its optimum level. A quiet, attentive mind, free of irrelevant distractions, is necessary for us to perform vigorous exercise in a truly beneficial manner. A relaxed and creative state of mind within a well-attuned body: this is the beginning and end of fitness, the optimum condition if we want to break free of ingrained attitudes, acquire new skills, and discover what true fitness can mean.

STEPS TO A NEW APPROACH

Here are a number of practical suggestions that can help to bring about a new sense of healthy exploration and enjoyment in the water. Characteristically, they act as reminders to ourselves to let go of habits that may have become quite automatic. Use them – singly, in groups, and all together – as promptings to self-exploration in the water. By letting go of the old habits, a better, more creative way of swimming can emerge.

Don't hold in your stomach or hunch your shoulders, before or on entering the water. It may be chilly, or others may be watching. But awareness of habits like this is important. The way you are before entering the water reflects and is bound to affect your disposition when you swim.

Avoid setting a target number of lengths and counting.
20 lengths, 50 lengths, what does it prove? It only takes your mind off the actual swimming. Why give yourself irrelevant orders? Dropping this often unconsidered habit can be truly liberating.

Don't hold your breath.
This is often unconscious, in which case you need to make it conscious, so that you can learn to avoid breathlessness and hyperventilation. There is rarely any merit in deliberately holding your breath. It's likely to disturb your ability to think clearly about what you're doing.

Don't tense or hyperextend your body.
These are two of the main causes of cramp. Both detract from the elegance and efficiency of a stroke, and detrimentally affect use inside and outside the water.

Don't fight the water.
You can only lose! Make the water your ally instead. Excessive effort is unnecessary and distracting, and in over-exerting yourself you fail to exploit the water's unique asset of buoyancy.

Don't rush, but enjoy each stroke.
A well-executed stroke is likely to have greater benefits for body-toning and aerobic build-up, as well as giving the space for mindful activity, than a flurry of movement made in the pursuit of a dubious fitness goal.

Pay attention to what you're doing without letting your mind wander.
It's a good idea to think about painting when you paint, and cooking when you cook. That way you paint and cook better, and enjoy yourself more in the process. So why not pay attention to your swimming when you swim?

Don't Compare
Why do you need to match your performance with other swimmers? There is nothing to be gained, and much to be lost, by adopting other peoples' unconsidered goals and practices. Be attentive to your own use and form, and leave others to their own styles and purposes.

Experiment.
You don't have to limit yourself to a set routine. Try something new.

Smile!
It's surprising how few swimmers are aware of the extent to which they tense up their facial muscles. Smiling can draw your attention to this as well as helping to relax your face – an index of how relaxed the rest of your body is.

Fig. 5.11   *There are many ways of enjoying the benefits of water*

CONCLUSION

*There is a Law of Reversed Effort. The harder we try with the conscious will
to do something, the less we shall succeed. Proficiency and the results
of proficiency come only to those who have learned the
paradoxical art of doing and not doing.*

Aldous Huxley

A common feature of the case histories in this chapter is the emphasis on trying
to achieve, the sort of end-gaining that invariably accompanies the unthinking
pursuit of fitness. We must be careful not to apply the same sort of trying to the
task of learning a new approach, thus replacing one form of end-gaining with
another. Alexander found that when pupils try to do the 'right thing' they are
inclined to apply the wrong sort of effort to the task, which actually prevents
them from performing it efficiently. In his Notes of Instruction we read: 'I don't
want you to give a damn if you're right or not. Directly you don't care if you're
right or not the impeding obstacle is gone.' Swimmers who try to 'do it the right
way' create tensions which serve only to restrict their movements in the water.
The anxiety aroused by trying to do the right thing is itself detrimental to awareness. The Alexander Technique shifts the emphasis away from trying to do the
right thing to learning to prevent the wrong.

Learning the art of swimming involves discovering how to control the body's
natural buoyancy and make it work for you. As the body has a lower density than
water, it will almost always float unless something is done to prevent it. Many
adult beginners are reluctant to let the water support them, and may think that
if they do nothing they will immediately sink to the bottom. Although there are
individual physical differences which make it easier for some people to float than
others, the main obstacle to floating is the false notion that the body must
actively be held up in the water. The idea of non-doing also applies in another
way. Swimming efficiently involves using the least effort to overcome resistance
from the water. Applying too much effort increases friction and turbulence.
Studies of Olympic swimmers have shown that the fastest swimmers are the
ones who take the fewest strokes to cover the distance. What counts is not the
amount of effort, but the appropriate use of effort. It can be interesting to see
how few strokes you need to take to swim a given distance without loss of
momentum.

The principle of non-doing was crucial to Helen's recognition (Case Study
5B, p. 129) that thrashing about wouldn't help her learn to float, let alone swim.
Non-doing is not the same as passivity or total inactivity. It's simply the result of

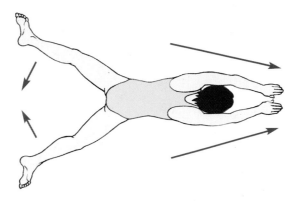

2. The ankles, knees and hip-joints rotate so that the feet are turned outwards at the width of the hips. Avoid starting this action from the knees,
   i.e. turning the knees out and keeping the feet together.

3. The thrust is generated through the hips into the thighs and knees. The
   legs should be directed evenly outwards and then immediately squeezed
   together. The kick should be symmetrical: an uneven kick in which one leg
   turns outward more than the other (a 'screw kick') can twist the hip and
   injure the spine (*Fig.* 5.8, p. 130). Pushing the heels back with excessive
   force can hurt the lower back.

Leg action:
The main propulsion in the breaststroke comes from the backward thrust followed
by the closing together of the legs. This is preceded by a phase in which the legs
are brought into the appropriate preparatory position for a safe and effective
thrust.

Arm action.
The main purpose of the arm action is to facilitate the inhalation. The arms also counteract the preparatory forward movement of the knees (no. 1 above), which would otherwise pull the body backwards.

1. As with the leg action the initial phase is non-propulsive. Let the arms open just beyond shoulder width. Think about the movement starting from the shoulders and spreading out to the arms and hands.

2. Leaving the wrists relaxed, scoop the arms down and round until the hands meet in front of the chest. Avoid snatching the arms in.

3. Extend the arms forward and down as the head goes back into the water. Pulling the arms upwards causes arching of the lower back.

Helpful hints

1. The most common reason why many adults have ineffective leg action is stiffness in the hips. Flexibility exercises on land are much more beneficial than exercising in the pool alone.

2. Kick-boards should not be used, as they place the body in an incorrect position which puts strain on the neck and back (*Fig. 5.14*).

It is inadvisable to emulate the style of competitive swimmers. Modern competitive breaststroke involves a vigorous body undulation, a forceful contraction of the shoulders, and a powerful whip kick. The shoulder shrug narrows the back, reducing resistance and taking advantage of the large pectoral and latissimus muscles. However, it also induces unhealthily rounded shoulders on land and a collapsed chest. The whip kick uses a leg action in which the knee rapidly rotates and the thighs snap together, generating power at the expense of pressure on the knee joint. While these actions can produce a powerful stroke, most adults do not have enough flexibility to perform them without injuring their backs. Even in highly agile athletes, this style of swimming often produces strain in the shoulders, neck and back.

FRONT CRAWL

A common fault is to use too much muscular effort when the arms moves through the air (the recovery) and not enough when they pull through the water. Excessive effort on the non-propulsive phase of the arm action is not only a waste of effort, it makes it harder to control the underwater arm action.

Fig 5.14 *Using a kick-board can cause strain to the lower back*

Traditional swimming coaching encourages a high, pitched elbow position for the recovery. Exaggerating this action can put the shoulders under strain. It is more comfortable for the arm to rotate gradually as it pulls through the the water so that the hand exits thumb first, then to bend the elbow as the arm comes forward over the water surface.

Fig 5.15 *Using a pull-buoy prevents the body from achieving natural boyancy*

Under the water, the elbow bends as the arm pulls back towards the body. This action creates the S-shaped pull spoken of in technical swimming manuals. On no account should one deliberately try to create an S-shaped pull. The attempt to do so has a distorting effect on one's orientation and disrupts the direction of the stroke. The main function of the legs is to keep the body balanced on both a horizontal and lateral axis. Kicking too fast or too vigorously can create an unbalanced stroke.

Helpful Hints

1. Practise shifting your balance to either side, starting with the hips.

2. Learn how to swim balanced to either side, kicking continuously.

3. On land, practise the arm movements, noting how the arm swivels naturally in the shoulder joint.

BACKSTROKE

Poor technique in backstroke can lead to shoulder strain and even tendonitis, which usually result from tensing the arm during the underwater phase of the stroke. The arm should never be held rigidly, but should be flexible and slightly bent at the elbow at all times.

---

1. Let the thumb lead as the arm comes out of the water, and the little finger as the arm goes back in.

2. Once the arm is below the surface, bend at the elbow rather than letting the arm remain extended.

3. Experiment with the angle of your head. With the head angled forward, it can be easier for the arms to generate leverage on the water, while a lower angle can aid balance and streamlining.

4. Maintain a central position for the head, neck and back throughout.

BUTTERFLY

In the butterfly, propulsion is created by both legs and arms. Inexperienced swimmers who attempt the stroke often pull back their arms violently and throw them back into the water. This is unnecessarily strenuous, causes undue turbulence, and can result in pain in the back and shoulders. The key to an efficient, streamlined butterfly stroke is to learn the dolphin-like undulation of the torso and the correct timing of arms and legs.

As in the crawl, more effort should be put into the pull, which starts once the arms have returned to the water, than the recovery. The legs work together from the hips, held firmly but not stiffly together, and free at the knees and ankles. The legs kick twice for every arm cycle. To maximize the benefits of good streamlining the head should remain below the surface for two arm cycles, with a breath being taken every two strokes.

FAIR WEATHER SWIMMERS

For people with busy lives who do not pursue for a regime of regular exercise, a holiday can provide the time to feel guilty about a year of inactivity. Access to the sea or to a good swimming pool and fitness activities can spur holiday-makers to a sudden burst of physical activity. Swimming is seen as offering the chance to cool down, sport new swimwear, tone muscles and improve general fitness. Unlike weight training or high impact aerobics, swimming is regarded as a safe vacational activity, with little risk of injury attendant on it. But a week of thrashing up and down in the water cannot make up for a year of inactivity, and often does more harm than good. It is therefore worth bearing in mind the following advice:

1. Start moderately, and gradually build up the time you swim each day.

2. Aim to enjoy the water rather than embark on a fitness regime.

3. Don't swim with your face out of the water. A holiday can be the perfect occasion to learn good orientation – and you don't have the excuse that there's no time to dry your hair.

4. Bring variety to your swimming – vary the stroke, distance and speed.

beyond the art of swimming

To plunge into water, to move one's whole body, from head to toe,
in its wild and graceful beauty; to twist about in its pure depths,
this is for me a delight only comparable to love.
Paul Valéry

Life-giving, cleansing, and endlessly abundant, water has nurtured humanity from the earliest times. When we swim, we are interacting with a medium that has exercised magical and spiritual associations for people since the dawn of history. In its myriad forms water has inspired poetry, art, literature, music, wonder, exploration, and love. In a world of dwindling ecological resources, it is a gift to value and cherish. The art of swimming cannot be complete without a profound appreciation of our connection as living beings to the wonderful, unique medium which is intertwined with every aspect of our existence. Water surrounds and embraces our lives with its awesome beauty and variety. We watch it, marvel at it, listen to it, bathe in it, drink it – and swim in it. According to ancient Egyptian legend, the gods bestowed the gift of water on humankind in recompense for enclosing us in a physical body. It was said that through our association with water we become connected to our spiritual nature, and our bodies might discover the freedom that our souls had lost. The Hebrews imagined water as a primordial element, present at the birth of all creation when 'the spirit of the Lord moved upon the face of the waters' (Genesis 1.2). The religions and mythology of Sumeria and Babylonia, of India and China, of peoples ranging from Australasia to the Americas, are replete with stories and symbolism which speak of reverence for water.

The ancient Greeks recognised water to be the source of life. They worshipped spirits of the water, and pondered deeply on its spiritual and physical qualities. Their myth, art, poetry and literature reflect on it and celebrate it in all its aspects. More than two and a half thousand years ago, Thales, one of the originators of the tradition of Western philosophical thought, identified water as the wellspring of all Being, the substance from which all things arose. Heraclitus used the image of water to demonstrate the ever-changing nature of the universe. 'Everything is in flux,' he stated, 'One cannot step into the same river twice.' The poet Pindar praised water in a famous line as being the 'noblest of all the elements.' And it was while bathing that Archimedes came upon his insight – immortalised by his exclamation 'Eureka!' – that a body's mass can be determined by the amount of water it displaces.

The value of learning to swim is emphasised in many societies and traditions. For the Greeks it was a civilised accomplishment, on a par with learning the alphabet as a basic element of education. They were proud of their ability to swim and dive, activities represented in their earliest literature, the epics of Homer. Swimming was not viewed as a competitive sport, and did not feature in the ancient Olympic Games. But the Greeks took for granted that it was a skill necessary for self-preservation, not least in the event of shipwreck (it was a notable irony that the outstanding military genius of the ancient world, Alexander the Great, was unable to swim). The Romans were explicit about the instruction of swimming, both for military purposes and for pleasure. In a line of Ovid, a Roman poet of the first century B.C. and a keen swimmer, we encounter the first occurrence of the phrase 'the art of swimming' (*ars nandi*). In the Jewish Talmud it is considered an obligation, as well as a good deed worthy of respect, for fathers to teach their sons how to swim. In many countries today, children are expected to be taught basic swimming skills by the time they have completed their primary education.

For aquatic creatures like fish, seals, and dolphins, swimming is not an art. But for human beings, relating to water as if it were our element demands art. Thinking of swimming as an art encourages us to cultivate the natural affinity that human beings have with the water. It's up to each individual how far we wish to develop that art for ourselves and incorporate it into our lives. Being at home in the water opens up a realm of possibilities which we can hardly contemplate if we are not familiar with the art of swimming. Aquatic activities such as snorkelling, diving, and swimming with dolphins, are exciting ways of discovering the underwater world and expanding our horizons through interaction with water.

HEALING POWER OF WATER

Water is both literally and symbolically the source of life. It's the most abundant substance on the surface of the Earth, covering more than 70% of the planet. It constitutes a large proportion of all living things: about two thirds of a human being's body mass is made up of water. To ensure the efficient functioning of our metabolism and bodily systems, we need to drink it in sufficient quantities every day. Water is a universal solvent, allowing us to assimilate the minerals and vitamins that are vital for strength and health. Insufficient liquid intake even affects the development of bone tissue, ultimately weakening the skeletal framework, reducing its plasticity, and bringing on conditions such as osteoporosis.

The restorative powers of water have been recognised and acclaimed for millennia. Hippocrates, the father of Western medicine, emphasised the importance of drinking for health and had a high regard for water's curative powers. The Greeks prescribed bathing in natural springs as a cure for disease and as a way of increasing vigour and vitality. They filled their town centres with springs and fountains, to give pleasure both to the eye and the ear. Their great medical sanctuaries dedicated to the god Asclepius were established around healing baths and fountains. The Romans went even further, seeking out natural springs wherever they ventured and erecting over them beautifully designed buildings, so that the Roman Bath (like its historical successor the Turkish Bath) is associated with opulence and tranquillity to this day.

Fig. 6.2   *Roman baths at Bath in western England*

Nowadays, water therapies of all kinds are widely used and increasingly popular throughout the world. Spas and hydros are centres for health breaks and convalescence, used in the rehabilitation of a wide range of physical and psychological conditions. Activity in water helps the recovery of wasted and injured muscles; patients who are too weak to move an injured limb without aid may be able to perform a full range of movement in a hydrotherapy pool. Warm baths can help to restore mobility, treat digestive problems, relieve insomnia and promote general muscular relaxation. Cold water is used to lower the body temperature, relieve muscular pains, boost poor circulation, treat skin conditions and reduce inflammations. Alongside therapies, there has increasing emphasis on recreational exercise conducted in water, such as the techniques of Ai Chi and Watsu. Whether associated with calmness and tranquillity, or strength and vitality, water has powerful effects on the human mind and spirit. It's well known that the sight and sound of the ocean, of a flowing river, or a cascading waterfall, elicit positive feelings. This is in part due to the actual physical properties of flowing water. At the sea-shore or by the side of a waterfall, there is an abundance of negative ions, which has been shown to have a beneficial effect on mind and body. The molecules of the air we breathe carry electrical charges which affect the functioning of cells throughout our body. An excess of positive ions, such as is found in most cities, has a fatiguing and debilitating effect.

Fig. 6.3   *Watsu: freeing the body in the water*

Even the sound of water – a running river or the lapping of waves – produces a measurable effect on our organism. Research has shown that when we listen to the sound of flowing or rushing water, wave patterns in our brain alter in a similar way to when we relax or meditate. Longer exposure to such sounds is used as a way of treating anxiety, tension and depression.

Why analyse and treat in isolation all these benefits that water has to offer when water is so abundant? Learn to be alive to the sound, sight and feel of water in all its natural, invigorating and life-enhancing wholeness. Become aware in the water of the inner rhythms of your body. Listen in the silence to your heartbeat as you float motionless. Celebrate the rhythm of your limbs as you swim. Learn to trust water, play with it, and appreciate its tremendous strength. Seek out the currents below the surface, rock gently in swelling waves, feel the water's silky caress on your skin, and submerge yourself in its embrace. In these ways you can discover for yourself the healing power of water.

REFLECTIONS ON WATER

Spiritual and religious associations with water are universal, and water has special associations for many faiths throughout the world. Water symbolises the cleansing of the spirit as well as the body, and this symbolism has frequently been incorporated into religious ritual. Bathing in the holy water of the ancient river Ganges is a religious duty for Hindus. Similarly, there is a religious aspect to bathing in Judaism, which was inherited by the Christian ritual of baptism. Since the 19th century, Catholics in their millions have also made pilgrimages to the sanctified waters of Lourdes in France, and thousands of visitors marvel at the holy springs and the tranquil pools around the Japanese temples to Buddha in the ancient capital of Kyoto.

In the philosophies of Zen and the Tao, the image of moving water is used as a symbol of the flowing, constantly changing nature of life. Water is gentle and yielding, yet possesses tremendous strength. 'Nothing in this world is softer than water, but nothing is better at overcoming the hard.' Water and its properties are profoundly connected with notions of balance and harmony. The words of the Tao reflect Oriental ideas of Yin and Yang, the complementary poles of cosmic force which interact to create the equilibrium of existence. For human beings, awareness of how to bring these elements into balance in our own lives is the key to health and happiness.

This book began with an exploration of awareness, and we have come full circle. Awareness of our self, of the way we stand, move, and breathe, has led us to explore how we relate to our bodies and to the water, and how we choose to lead our lives. We have suggested that the art of swimming can be a source of self-discovery, personal growth and empowerment. A new approach to the water – one which teaches us to be aware of ourselves, to relate it to our organic wholeness and balance, to be at home in the water, to understand and make use of its generous properties, to discover its intimate connections with the rhythms of our life – awakens in us the possibility of a wealth of hitherto unexperienced sensation, and the discovery of unprecedented, indefinable joy.

can water be a friend?

by Daphne Wood

she went into the water
like going to meet a friend
the water received her
as she was
demanded nothing
but was not unresponsive
allowed her to be tense
reflected that back to her
encouraged her to let some of her holding
be let go
responded when she did
seemed to become softer
and gentler
surrounding her
holding her

as she learned more about the water
and responded
she learned more about herself
perhaps coming into the water
was more like coming back to herself

it was also more than that
the water may not remember and think about her as a friend would
but knowing it would be there
constant
reliable
made her look forward to going to the water
as she would to going to a friend.

further reading

Ai Chi – Balance Harmony & Healing: Ruth Sova with Jun Konno; DSL, 1999

Alexander Technique as I See It: Patrick Macdonald; Rahula Books; 1989

The Alexander Technique in Everyday Life (formerly titled *Body Know-how*):
   Jonathan Drake; Thorsons, 1996

Aquatic Exercise: Ruth Sova; DSL,1992

The Art of Running: Malcolm Balk & Andrew Shields; Ashgrove, 2000

Body Learning: Michael Gelb; Aurum Press, 1994

The Complete Guide to Exercise in Water (YMCA): Debbie Lawrence; A. & C. Black, 2000

The Complete Illustrated Guide to the Alexander Technique: Glyn McDonald; Element, 1998

Discover the Underwater World – Book and Video for Snorkelling:
   International Padi Inc., 1999

Dolphin Healing: Horace Dobbs; Piatkus, 2000

*F. Matthias Alexander The Man and His Work – Memoirs of Training in the Alexander
   Technique 1931-34*: Lulie Westfeldt; Centerline Press, 1964,1998

Fitness Swimming: Emmet Hines; Human Kinetics, 1999

Flow in Sports: Susan A. Jackson & Mihaly Csikszentmihalyi; Human Kinetics, 1999

Freedom to Change – The Development and Science of the Alexander Technique:
   Frank Pierce Jones, ed; J.M.O. Fischer; Mouritz, 1997

Go Dive – Manual and Video for Scuba Diving: International Padi Inc., 1995

Haunts of the Black Masseur: Charles Sprawson; Vintage, 1993

Hydrotherapy: Margaret Reid Campion; Butterworth-Heinemann, 1996

Mind and Muscle – An Owner's Handbook: Elizabeth Langford; Garant Uitgevers, 1999

Self-help Alexander Technique Handbook: Chris Stevens; Vermilion, 1997

Sensitive Chaos – The Creation of Flowing Forms in Water and Air: Theodor Schwenk;
   Anthroposophic Press; 1990

Swimming Past 50: Mel Goldstein & Dave Tanner; Human Kinetics, 1998

Thinking Aloud – Talks on Teaching the Alexander Technique: Walter Carrington,
   Mornum Press, 1994

Total Swimming: Harvey Wiener: Simon and Schuster, 1980

The Use of the Self: F. Matthias Alexander; Gollancz, 1932, 1985

Water – Pure Therapy: Alice Kavounas; Kyle Cathie, 2000

Water Log – A Swimmer's Journey through Great Britain: Roger Deakin; Vintage, 2000

Watsu – Freeing the Body in Water: Harold Dull; Harbin Springs, 1997

Zen in the Art of Archery: Eugene Herrigel; Arkana, 1990

useful addresses

AMSAT
American Society for the
Alexander Technique
P.O. Box 60008
Florence, MA 01062 USA
Telephone: (+1) 800-473-0620

Amateur Swimming Association (UK)
Harold Fern House
Derby Square
Loughborough LE11 5AL
UK
Telephone: (+44) (0)1509-618700
Email: cserv@asagb.org.uk

ASCA
American Swimming Coaches Association
2101 North Andrews Avenue, Suite 107
Fort Lauderdale
Florida 33311 USA
Telephone: (+1) 954-563-4930

Aqua Mouvance,
7595 De Gaspé
Montréal, Québec H2R 2A3
Canada
(+1) 514-948-5709
Email: aqua@cam.org

Halliwick Association for
Swimming Therapy
Education Secretary c/o ADKC Centre
Whitstable House
Silchester Rd
London W10 6SB
UK

The Henning Library at the Inter-
national Swimming Hall of Fame
One, Hall of Fame Drive
Fort Lauderdale, FL 33316 USA
Telephone: (+1) 954-462-6536, Ext. 204
Fax: (+1) 954-522-4521

Hilary Austin, Watsu Practitioner
and AT teacher
26 Tudor Gardens
Middlesex TW1 4LE
UK
Telephone: (+44) (0)208-8929154
Email: hydrohilary@yahoo.com

International Dolphin Watch
10 Melton Rd
North Ferriby
East Yorkshire HU14 3ET
UK
Email: idw@talk21.com

PADI (Americas)
Professional Association
of Diving Instructors
30151 St Thomas Street
Rancho Santa Margarita
CA 92688 USA
(+1) 800-729-7234

PADI International (UK)
Unit 7, St Philips Central
Albert Road
St Philips, Bristol BS2 OPD UK
Telephone: (+44) (0)117-3007234
Fax: (+44) (0)117-9710400

RLSS

  The Royal Life Saving Society

River House, High Street

Broom,

Warwickshire B50 4HN

Telephone: (+44) (0)1789 773994

Fax: (+44) (0)1789 773995

STA

  Swimming Teachers' Association

Anchor House, Birch Street

Walsall WS2 8HZ

UK

Telephone: (+44) (0)1922 645097

STAT

  Society of Teachers of the
  Alexander Technique

1st Floor, Linton House

39-51 Highgate Road

London NW5 1RS

Telephone: (+44) (0)20 7284 3338

WABA

  Worldwide Aquatic Bodywork Association

P.O. Box 889, Middletown,

CA 95461 USA

Telephone (+1) 707-987-3801

Fax (+1) 707-987-9638

credits

Photography and Drawings: Andy Lane, page 32, 71, 80-1, 87, 98-9, 102-3, 106-7, 110-2, 115, 122, 130, 133, 137; Allsport 12, 74-5, 89, 124; Hilary Austin, 148; Walter Carrington 16, 19; Tim Hill, 108; Jessica Johnson 38; Laboratory Spa & Health Club 36, 65, 117; Sophia Lewis, 55; Jill McArthur 23, 43, 66, 77, 119, 131; Ken McMullen, 149; Bipinchandra J Mistry, 144, 150; Linda Price, 51, 140; Carl Stringer, 46; Caroline Swatton, 78, 79; Julian Warner 14, 25, 41, 46, 59, 60, 67, 88, 91, 121, 123; Dawn Watts, 135; Anne Wodmoore 138-9. Text: Daphne Wood, page 151, *Can Water be a Friend?*

Andy Lane is a professional photographer specialising in people and portraiture. His fascination with water began at an early age. He spent part of his childhood on the island of Malta, obsessed with snorkelling and the sea. Now a scuba diving enthusiast, he has created a wide range of underwater imagery and sees his pictures of swimmers as a new focus of his work.

Jill McArthur has created award-winning photographic images of women for the *Sunday Times* colour supplement. She is particularly interested in photographing the human body in all its aspects.

Julian Warner is an artist who lives and works in London. He is an anatomical draughts-man and illustrator and has studied the Alexander Technique.

acknowledgements

This book, now revised and thoroughly reset, has always exceeded expectations of the time and commitment needed for its production. We are grateful to all who have assisted in its creation and contributed to its continuing success. Our thanks remain due to Robin Campbell for first publishing the book in Ashgrove's 'Art of…' series and thereby deciding us on its title. We again gratefully acknowledge the earlier contributions of Helen and Laura Allen, Sarah Barnet, Sharon Berry, George Blair, Walter Carrington, Lea Clark, Horace Dobbs, Eileen Emmerton, Georgina Evans, Denyse Faulkner, Odyssée Gaveau, Jamie Gayle, Laurence Gerlis, Jane Goss, Tomoe Inoue, Adam Jackson, Terry Laughlin, Angus McArthur, Ken McMullen, Nina Meyer, Edna Perlman, Peter Rowlands, Chloë Stallibrass, Rita Shamia, Robert Smith, Oliver Suralli, Zeev Tadmor, Deborah Taylor, and Sue and Simon Trewin. To these should now be added Hilary Austin, Kenneth Bass, Anthony Cantle, Ruby Clough, Ian and Maggie Cross, Neil Friedland, Vicky Harmer, Irene Jacob, Jessica Johnson, Lawrence Kershen, Jun Konno, Tara Lemon, Lev the photographer, Sophia Lewis, Sam Neville, Linda, Rachel and Robin Price, Andrew Shields, Yohai Shoresh, Caroline Swatton, Dawn Watts, David Wilkie, Daphne Wood, Mayumi Yanu, and Holly the Dolphin. We are grateful for the enthusiastic interest and endorsement of numerous societies and organisations (including some of those listed on pages 153-4) concerned with the Alexander Technique, swimming, and other therapeutic and water-related activities.

We reiterate our thanks to artist and illustrator Julian Warner and photographer Jill McArthur, who have together provided many of the book's enduring images; and to Andrew Barker and John Lyras, together with the staff of the Laboratory Spa and Health Club, London, for their ongoing and consistent support. Thanks again to Victoria Wood for her pointed and witty foreword. Special thanks to Andy Lane for his excellent underwater images for this new edition, and to Oceanic for the use of their underwater film studio.

Helen and Maurice Shaw have tirelessly assisted this project from the outset. They and our respective partners, Limor and Karen, and the children Talia and Tomer, have our thanks for their help, patience and support. Finally, our thanks go to our publisher Brad Thompson for his unflagging efforts in the design and production of this attractive new edition.

information

INSTRUCTION

For information about our one-to-one lessons, weekly courses, day workshops, swimming holidays in the UK and abroad, teacher training or for a list of teachers of the Shaw Method, contact us at:

Shaw Method Limited
27 Greenway Close
London N20 8ES
Tel:(+44) (0)20 8446 9442
Fax:(+44) (0)20 8632 9570
Email: info@artofswimming.com
Website: www.artofswimming.com

VIDEOS

Art of Swimming Video
This video, filmed in beautiful locations in the Red Sea, is an inspirational adventure into the art of swimming. The viewer will discover the joys of swimming breaststroke, crawl and backstroke – all without strain The original insights offered are supported by demonstrations and interviews with Olympic Gold Medalist David Wilkie, Japanese team coach Jun Konno and international actress Irene Jacobs.
Now available in both PAL and NTSC formats.
Price £12.99 or $25.00 plus p&p

New Shaw Method Steps
This tape shows the progression of the series of integrated steps to establish a healthier and more efficient way of swimming. Instruction is given in the breaststroke, front crawl and backstroke. The tape also gives guidance on working with a partner, which is particularly suitable for teachers and coaches.
*Now available in both PAL and NTSC formats.*Price £10.95 plus p&p

index

Page numbers in **bold** print indicate illustrations

Published in Great Britain by ASHGROVE PUBLISHING
an imprint of HOLLYDATA PUBLISHERS LTD
55 Richmond Avenue
London N1 0LX

First published 1996, Reprinted 1996, 1997
Revised Edition 1998, Reprinted 1998, 2000
New Edition 2001, Reprinted 2003

ISBN 1-85398-140 0

Book Design by Brad Thompson
Printed and bound in Malta by Interprint